MAKING THE MOST OF YOUR COLLEGE EXPERIENCES

A Guide for Communication Majors

DIANE M. MONAHAN, PHD
Saint Leo University

Bassim Hamadeh, CEO and Publisher
Todd R. Armstrong, Publisher
Anne Jones, Project Editor
Alia Bales, Associate Production Manager
Jess Estrella, Senior Graphic Designer
Alexa Lucido, Licensing Manager
Natalie Piccotti, Director of Marketing
Kassie Graves, Senior Vice President, Editorial
Jamie Giganti, Director of Academic Publishing

Copyright © 2024 by Cognella, Inc. All rights reserved. No part of this publication may be reprinted, reproduced, transmitted, or utilized in any form or by any electronic, mechanical, or other means, now known or hereafter invented, including photocopying, microfilming, and recording, or in any information retrieval system without the written permission of Cognella, Inc. For inquiries regarding permissions, translations, foreign rights, audio rights, and any other forms of reproduction, please contact the Cognella Licensing Department at rights@cognella.com.

Trademark Notice: Product or corporate names may be trademarks or registered trademarks and are used only for identification and explanation without intent to infringe.

Cover image copyright © 2014 Depositphotos/fffranzzz.
Design images copyright © 2019 Depositphotos/MMVector.

Printed in the United States of America.

BRIEF CONTENTS

Introduction   1

Part I   You Are the Key to Your Own Success

Chapter 1   It's Never Too Early to Think About Your Career   5

Chapter 2   Identifying Your Values, Interests, and Skills   21

Chapter 3   Building Your Personal Brand   53

Part II   The Business of Communication

Chapter 4   Aligning Your Goals   73

Chapter 5   Choosing a Career in Communication   97

Chapter 6   Advice You Can Use From Faculty   109

Chapter 7   Finding Your Seat on the Bus   123

Chapter 8   Industry Advice   135

Part III   From Internship to Employment

Chapter 9   Finding and Preparing for Your Internship   147

Chapter 10   Top 10 "Must Dos" During Your Internship   161

Chapter 11   Let's Get Real   177

DETAILED CONTENTS

About the Author   xi
Preface   xiii

Introduction   1

Part I   You Are the Key to Your Own Success

Chapter 1   It's Never Too Early to Think About Your Career   5

       The Reason for General Education Requirements   6
       Finding the Competitive Advantage in General Education   8
       The Role of the Academic Advisor   14
       Key Terms   18

Chapter 2   Identifying Your Values, Interests, and Skills   21

       Values Guide Your Future Career   23
       Interests Add Color to Your Work   26
       What Is Your Skillset?   34
       Key Terms   49

Chapter 3   Building Your Personal Brand   53

       Creating a Personal Brand   53
       Creating a Presence on Social Media   60
       Creating a Video Cover Letter   65
       Building a Portfolio of Evidence of Employability   66
       Key Terms   69

Part II   The Business of Communication

Chapter 4   Aligning Your Goals   73

       SMART and SMARTE Goals   73
       Personal SWOT   89

Debriefing   92
Key Terms   95

Chapter 5   Choosing a Career in Communication   97

Carter: A Case Study   97
Advantages of a Communication Degree   102
Key Terms   107

Chapter 6   Advice You Can Use From Faculty   109

Knowing Available Resources and Using Them   109
Connecting With Faculty and Staff   112
Making the Most of Teamwork and Communication   113
Creating Your Personal Brand   116
Investing in Others   117
International Experiences   118
Job Interview Preparation and Expectations   119
Strategically Use Internships   119
Get Involved   120
Skills Expectations   121

Chapter 7   Finding Your Seat on the Bus   123

Being a Bus Rider   124
Getting on the Right Bus   127
Key Terms   133

Chapter 8   Industry Advice   135

Mandy Menaker   136
Amanda Ponzar   137
Stacy Sherman   138
Colby Reade   139
Tom Wozniak   140
Alastair McCapra   140
Charlie Terenzio   141
Paul Rhynard   142

Part III From Internship to Employment

Chapter 9 Finding and Preparing for Your Internship 147

Experiential Learning 149
The Nature of Internships 151
Finding Your Internship 152
Preparing for Your Internship 156
Key Terms 160

Chapter 10 Top 10 "Must Dos" During Your Internship 161

Make a First Impression 162
Make Connections 166
Be Professional 168
Have Learning Objectives 169
Ask Questions 170
Find Opportunities to Shine 171
Take Notes 172
Adapt to the Business Culture 173
Explore 174

Chapter 11 Let's Get Real 177

Expectations vs. Reality 177
Job Hunting 185
Keeping Your Head Up 187
Go Forth and Conquer 189

Glossary 191
References 197
Index 203

SPOTLIGHTS, EXERCISES, & TOOLS

SPOTLIGHTS ON COMMUNICATION

Cognitive Scripts	10
Mentoring	15
Identity	46
Elaboration Likelihood Model	55
Communication Strategy	92
Organizational Culture	102
The Learning Organization Theory	110
Organizational Systems Theory	131
Constructivism	135
Narrative Theory	158
Impression Management	166
Constructivism	182

EXERCISES

1.1 Building a Base of Knowledge	11
1.2 Creating a Habit of Asking Meaningful Questions	13
2.1 Assessing Your Core Values	24
2.2 Your Work Values Story	26
2.3 Identifying Your Interests	28
2.4 Working With Your Interests	33
2.5 Conducting a Skills Gap Analysis	44
3.1 You As a Product	54
3.2 Finding Value in Companies' Mission Statements	58
3.3 Building Your Personal Brand	60
3.4 Creating Social Media Content	64
4.1 Lessons From the Coca-Cola SWOT Analysis	76
4.2 Lessons From the Zara SWOT Analysis	77
4.3 Lessons From the Apple SWOT Analysis	79
4.4 Lessons From Rachel's SWOT Analysis	82
4.5 Lessons from Marco's SWOT Analysis	84
4.6 Lessons From Tyrone's SWOT Analysis	86
4.7 Lessons From Mai's SWOT Analysis	88
4.8 Personal SWOT Analysis	91
5.1 Using the Occupational Outlook Handbook	100
6.1 Prompts for Finding Resources	112
6.2 Prompts for Connecting With Faculty and Staff	113
6.3 Prompts for Demonstrating Teamwork and Communication	115
6.4 Prompts for Establishing a Personal Brand	116
6.5 Prompts for Investing in Others	117
6.6 Prompts for Having International Experiences	118
6.7 Prompts for Thinking About Internships	120
6.8 Prompts for Getting Involved	121
6.9 Prompts for Collecting Skills	121
7.1 What Organizational Position Are You Best Suited For?	129
7.2 Describing Your Bus	130
8.1 Prompts for Action	137
8.2 Prompts for Action	138
8.3 Prompts for Action	139
8.4 Prompts for Action	139
8.5 Prompts for Action	140
8.6 Prompts for Action	141
8.7 Prompts for Action	141
8.8 Prompts for Action	143
9.1 Writing Learning Objectives for Your Internship	150
9.2 Developing Your 30-Second Elevator Pitch	155
9.3 Preparing for Common Interview Questions	158
10.1 Making a Positive First Impression	164
10.2 Making the Most of Internships	168
10.3 Becoming a Trusted Member of an Organization	168
10.4 Challenging Yourself	169
10.5 Managing Organizational Culture	173
11.1 The Connected Professional Project	178

TOOLS

For Thinking About Your Career Early	16
For Gaining Insight in Yourself	48
For a New Generation	67
For Aligning Your Goals	94
For Learning About Careers in Communication	106
For Advice You Can Use From Faculty	122
For Finding Your Seat on the Bus	132
For Thinking About Advice From the Industry	143
For Getting an Internship	159
For Exceeding in Your Internship	175
For Post-Graduation Expectations	190

WEB-BASED RESOURCES: ACCESSING QR CODES & LINKS

The author has selected some supporting web-based content for further engagement with the learning material that appears in this text, which can be accessed through QR codes or web links. These codes are intended for use by those who have purchased print copies of the book. You may scan them using a QR code reading app on your phone, which will take you to each website. You can also search for the link using a web browser search engine. Readers who have purchased a digital copy of the book can simply click on the hyperlinks beneath each QR code.

Cognella maintains no responsibility for the content nor availability of third-party links. However, Cognella makes every effort to keep its texts current. Broken links may be reported to studentreviews@cognella.com. Please include the book's title, author, and 7-digit SKU reference number (found below the barcode on the back cover of the book) in the body of your message.

Please check with your professor to confirm whether your class will access this content independently or collectively.

ABOUT THE AUTHOR

Diane M. Monahan, PhD

Dr. Diane Monahan serves as the chair of the Department of Communication, Hospitality, Marketing and Sport Business in the Tapia College of Business at Saint Leo University. She joined the Saint Leo University faculty in the fall of 2010. She holds a Bachelor of Science in Psychology from Florida State University, a Master of Arts in Communication from the University of Central Florida, and a Doctorate in Communication Sciences with emphasis on organizational communication and conflict management and cognate areas of social psychology (emphasis on aggression and violence) and Quantitative Methods from Temple University in Philadelphia.

At Saint Leo University she teaches undergraduate courses in communication and graduate courses in business. At the undergraduate level she has taught courses such as Interpersonal Communication, Crisis Communication, Organizational Communication, Intercultural Communication, and Communication Theory. At the graduate level she has taught Professional Development and Marketing Storytelling and Crisis Management in the Master of Business Administration program. In the Doctorate of Business Administration program she has taught Quantitative Research Methods, Organizational Behavior, and Dissertation Seminar. Elsewhere she has taught courses including Business and Professional Communication, Conflict Management, Small Group Communication, Decision Making Theory, Research Methods, Nonverbal Communication, and Dark Side of Interpersonal Communication, to list a few.

She has served as a consultant for nonprofit and for-profit organizations, improving communication with stakeholders, conducting communication audits, improving conflict culture, and identifying risk factors for workplace aggression. Her professional and research interests can be categorized into three broad areas: (1) interpersonal processes within organizations, such as conflict and workplace aggression; (2) organizational systems that impact employees, such a conflict systems and culture; and (3) instructional communication, such as how communication helps create effective learning communities and assessment of learning communities or programs. She has recently contributed two book chapters to two separate edited volumes.

PREFACE

A 2021 study by the Cengage Group of 1,600 recent college graduates reveals that graduates report they felt underqualified for starting their careers. Students also reported that they believe their universities did not provide them with needed job skills. There is evidence that when faculty talk to students about careers, students' confidence increases (Strada-Gallup, 2018). The more deliberate we are in incorporating conversations about entering the workforce upon graduation, the more students are prepared and successful. For example, when teaching intercultural communication class, I show job advertisements for open positions related to topics we are discussing in class. I use introductory classes and advising sessions to inform students how to strategically approach their college experience. In most cases a degree, a piece of paper, is not what will help them land a job; rather, the experiences they have while earning the diploma is what employers are looking for.

The purpose of this book is to provide guidance to communication majors for capitalizing on their college experiences. It presents intentional conversations about subjects that plan a role in being both prepared and successful when entering the workforce and communication professions. I am thrilled to present an important tool in creating meaningful dialogue with communication students focused on their success not only in college but, more importantly, after graduation. Helping students understand the value of their entire college experience provides added value to their diploma.

I recommend using the book as a resource for any introduction to communication course and then threading its contents throughout all levels of communication courses, such as career preparation, internships courses, and portfolios. The book is also a perfect addition to academic advising.

Why This Book?

This book provides a roadmap for students to follow as they discover themselves and their career goals. As a communication instructor I experienced a rude awakening when a communication major was interviewed by a campus member about the importance of writing across the curriculum. I was a new faculty member at the university, and I expected the student to share my opinion that strong writing skills were essential to be an effective communication professional. To my horror, the student stated that she did not do much writing, and it was not a very important skill for communication majors. Things changed and changed fast. Not only did I update the courses to include more connections to careers, I made it a mission to ensure that communication majors knew the relationship between writing and the communication field. I developed much of the content in this book as I built a sophomore-level course that equipped students with tools and information to see connections beyond courses to their intended careers.

I am not the only communication instructor who has heard students have a difficult time describing what communication is. The broadness of the major and field presents challenges to students being able to confidently name and describe what they want to do after graduation. Unless your program has a narrow focus, most faculty see students as being uncertain about their prospects after graduation. It is important to give students the tools to become more confident in how they will use their degree to be successful in the workforce and the communication industry.

Students often compartmentalize their college activities (e.g., general education or required courses, major courses, and social activities), missing the opportunity to demonstrate potential valuable job skills. There are many books that discuss the internship process, but this usually occurs at the end of a student's college career. Internships are discussed in this book, yet a broader, more encompassing approach to career readiness is included in the discussions. This book gives students the tools to use experiences in the classroom, as well as outside the classroom, as career building blocks. It highlights how students can apply communication even to activities and assignments outside of the communication field by focusing on transferable and power skills.

How Can This Book Serve as a Tool to Create More Confident Communication Majors?

One valuable feature of this book is that it takes what you may be talking about in class and connects it to getting a job. Let's face it, most students love their majors; this is no exception for communication majors. They were drawn to the major because of the material discussed in classes and the experiential learning opportunities weaved into many of the classes. With its deliberate connection to communication theory and concepts, this book can help students see the usefulness of what they are learning beyond the classroom. The recurring Spotlight on Communication feature focuses on discussions of concepts and theories as they relate to career readiness and job acquisition. Students can become more confident communication majors when they are able to provide a plan for getting a job. Feeling employable yields hope for the future, which results in confident majors!

Organization and Content

The structure of the chapters uses the following format: tell, show, do, and reflect. The discussions not only provide information but also examples that show how the concepts live in the students' lives and connect to communication research. The discussions lead into opportunities for the students to practice and use the information discussed. In addition to timely topics, the book provides several activities for students to complete, all with the intention of helping them build a strategy for being workplace-ready graduates. Resources for further reading, viewing, and reflecting are provided at the end of each chapter.

The book is divided into three parts, focusing on the student's sense of self, communication industry, and career.

Part I: You Are the Key to Your Own Success focuses on the student. These three chapters provide students with self-reflection and discovery of their interests, values, and skills. Understanding one's self will enable students to realize the need to lay the foundation on which they can build a future career. Each of these chapters takes a deeper look at concepts that form the building blocks of the emerging professional.

- Chapter 1: "It's Never Too Early to Think About Your Career" introduces general education requirements and how students can use these courses to create a competitive advantage for entering the workforce. Instruction is provided for asking different types of questions to critically think about topics. A discussion on academic advisors and how to utilize advising sessions for more than scheduling classes is also provided. The Spotlight on Communication introduces cognitive scripts. Cognitive scripts are used to help students understand how they process, store, and use information. The more students are exposed to event frames and social roles, the more agile they will be in adapting to different contexts.

- Chapter 2: "Identifying Your Values, Interests and Skills" focuses on students identifying three types of information about themselves: their values, interests, and skills. Effective communication and levels of competence are discussed. The Spotlight on Communication introduces identity, which includes our identity includes values, interests, and skills. Through the discussion of identity students see a connection between these three elements, helping them identify career possibilities.

- Chapter 3: "Building Your Personal Brand" introduces what a personal brand is and why students should begin creating one early in their college career. A deeper look into how to effectively use social media not only to build and promote their brand but also to connect with professionals and experts is explored. Students are instructed on creating a video cover letter a portfolio. The Spotlight on Communication introduces the elaboration likelihood model. The ELM is a great tool to help students connect communication theory with persuasion. The chapter discussed how a personal brand is only as good as its persuasive power. Being strategic and purposive, students are equipped with the tools to build and evaluate their personal brand's effectiveness using the ELM.

Part II: The Business of Communication includes five chapters focused how employing concepts from business, such as the SWOT analysis, can help students become more strategic in using the resources around them. Students are often overwhelmed, or even unaware, of opportunities available to graduates holding a bachelor's degree in communication. This part also provides career insights from both communication faculty and practitioners as well as shares advice from faculty and industry and helps students incorporate it into their lives as college students and thereafter.

- Chapter 4: "Aligning Your Goals" introduces the idea of SMARTE goals, with an emphasis on creating goals that are elevating and take students to the next place on their journey. The SWOT analysis is introduced and used to exemplify how to become more strategic about the future. The SWOT analysis is presented as a tool for students to identify their own strengths, weaknesses, opportunities, and threats. The Spotlight on Communication introduces communication strategy. Students are shown how strategic communication is a way of persuading other people to accept your ideas in the pursuit of accomplishing a goal. Students are asked to examine their personal SWOT analysis and how it aligns with building communication strategy.

- Chapter 5: "Choosing a Career in Communication" provides a closer look at the many careers under the communication umbrella. Students are introduced to the occupational outlook, and the advantages of a communication degree are discussed. The Spotlight on Communication introduces organizational culture. Understanding that not all organizations are the same is an important realization for students preparing to launch their career. Organizational culture is introduced to provide a framework for assessing the workplaces for fit.

- Chapter 6: "Advice You Can Use From Faculty" highlights faculty and their advice for the undergraduate college student. The advice focuses on using the opportunities during college to their full advantage. The Spotlight on Communication introduces learning organization theory. Learning organization is commonly referred to as a group of people who are continually enhancing their capabilities to reach a goal. Students can adopt this approach to their own personal education and how they approach learning.

- Chapter 7: "Finding Your Seat on the Bus" introduces Jim Collins's metaphor of the bus and finding your seat on the right bus. The chapter helps students become more focused on their future career and provides tools for continual assessment of their organizational life, even after landing their first job in their career field. The Spotlight on Communication introduces organizational systems theory. Systems theory is introduced to help students view work as done in the environment of an organization. An organization is a set of interdependent parts, each with its own specific function and interrelated responsibilities. The magic of organizations is what happens among the people. Understanding the importance of finding the organization that best fits will help students become successful employees.

- Chapter 8: "Industry Advice" highlights industry professionals who share advice for the college student and emerging professional. Students are prompted to reflect on the advice and how they might use it in their current lives. Students articulate how they can act on the advice. There is no Spotlight on Communication in this chapter; instead, you have the opportunity to connect the industry-related advice to your specific program's approach to communication. I recognize that if you are teaching in a mass communication major the connection from industry to communication theory will differ from if you are teaching in a rhetorical communication program. This provides you the opportunity to customize the spotlight. Consider asking students to develop their own spotlight to communication.

Part III: From Internship to Employee educates students on the process of gaining a valuable internship opportunity as well as steps for getting a job upon graduation.

- Chapter 9: "Finding and Preparing for Your Internship" provides strategies and tips for locating a competitive internship and how to best prepare for the interview process. The Spotlight on Communication introduces narrative theory. Understanding the interview process from the narrative theory is valuable for students. The theory provides a perspective on how experiences shape the stories they tell during interviews. Stories should align with the job.

- Chapter 10: "Top 10 'Must Dos' During Your Internship" highlights the top tactics student interns should take advantage of to make the most of their internship, thereby increasing the likelihood that they land a full-time job in the field of communication. The Spotlight on Communication introduces impression management. The literature on impression management is a great complement for reinforcing the process of how others see you.

- Chapter 11: "Let's Get Real: What to Expect Upon Graduation" discusses the nature of work. An activity called The Connected Professional is presented to students as a tool to learn more about the first days, months, and year after graduation. The Spotlight on Communication introduces constructivism. With the knowledge of constructivism, students can reflect on the connected professional exercise they completed in the chapter. The process of talking with established professionals in the career or industry they are interested in provides information that will require students to either assimilate or accommodate.

In short, *Making the Most of Your College Experiences: A Guide for Communication Majors* is structured to support in-class discussion about approaching the college years in a strategic manner. Throughout the book there are activities, and examples, resources for further exploration, which can all be used in the classroom. The contents provide a logic-based approach to coaching students to be active participants in their college education. It is a how-to guide and provides directions for what students should consider throughout their college journey to be the most successful upon graduation.

Acknowledgments

Without the hundreds of students I have taught, this book would not be. Each time I step inside a classroom I feel privileged. It is this privilege that makes me want to always strive to evolve as an instructor.

I would like to acknowledge and give my warmest thanks to the late Dr. Ross Brinkert of Pennsylvania State University, Abington. I will be ever grateful for his encouragement to write this book. His memory will be with me always. I would also like to acknowledge my colleagues at Saint Leo University, who not only provided support but provided content for the faculty advice chapter. I work with the best colleagues.

I would like to thank my editor, Todd Armstrong, who made this work possible. His guidance and advice carried me through all the stages of writing my project, including illness and a global pandemic. He never gave up on me.

Special thanks to Jessica D. McCall (The University of North Carolina at Greensboro) and Julia Crouse Waddell (West Chester University) for reviewing a draft of the book and providing invaluable feedback.

I would also like to give special thanks to my husband, Dirk, and my children, Maggie, Molly, Max, and Camden, for their continuous support and understanding when I was writing. Their support and room service sustained me through the months of writing.

Introduction

This is an exciting time in your life. You have arrived at college and are ready to have new experiences. You have decided to major in communication, or perhaps you are exploring the major. Many thoughts will likely run through your mind as you embark on this journey. You might have already started thinking about your desired career. It is not uncommon to be fielding questions about what you will do after college and what type of career you want and for these thoughts to spin in your head. If I may give some advice: Enjoy everything that college has to offer. It is a time of exploration.

Don't lose sight that you are starting this journey because of the promises it holds at the end of it. In any journey, planning is a must. The purpose of this book is to provide guidance for capitalizing on your college experiences. It presents intentional conversations about subjects that play a role in being both prepared and successful when entering the workforce and the communication professions. At the end of this book you will be better prepared and confident in your answers regarding what happens after graduation.

This book gives you the tools to use experiences in the classroom, as well as outside the classroom, as career building blocks. The strategy and tactics presented in this book will equip you with tools and information for seeing connections between courses and to your intended career. I'll guide you through important topics necessary to consider now, in the early days of your degree. The discussions are all about you. Taking small steps to create a strategy throughout your years in college will make you a workplace-ready graduate.

No matter where you are in your educational journey it is never too soon to think about your future after graduation, and this book provides a roadmap for doing just that. The first three chapters walk you through self-discovery, which provide you a foundation and context for your educational journey. Tactics are provided for learning to think more strategically about your new college experiences (Chapter 1). Candid conversation about topics that matter, such as your values, interests, and skills, are connected to your plans for a career path (Chapter 2). It is valuable to recognize that creating a personal brand is important during the era of social media. We will walk through the process of thinking about, deciding, and designing your personal brand. The first part of the book concludes with learning about personal brands and digital footprints. Using your own coursework, you will use social media, podcasts, and other venues to connect with others in the field as well as showcase your work.

The second part of the book focuses on making a plan and identifying actions you can take throughout your college experience to reach your goals, using concepts from business that can help you become more strategic in using resources around you. One vital component of building a strategy is having goals, and Chapter 4 introduces SMARTE goals (which is my take on the popular SMART goals acronym). Goals are fantastic, but to get the most of them you need to select ones that will take you to the next step in your journey. This conversation is extended in Chapter 5 with the examination of career options in the field of communication. The communication degree is among the most conferred degrees of undergraduates. It is popular because of the expansive foundation it provides in messaging. Communication is a degree that is attractive to employers across industries. You will take an inside look at what other instructors are telling their students about being successful in and after college (Chapter 6). With a better idea of your career interests you will be coached how to assess your place in an organization (Chapter 7). The final chapter (8) in this part shares advice from professionals across industries. I will coach you on taking action on the advice provided by professionals.

The final part of the book includes chapters that will help you transition from being a college student to an invaluable worker—from intern to employee. I'll walk you through finding and preparing for an internship (Chapter 9). For communication majors, internships are vital experiential learning opportunities that connect you directly with an industry and business. You will be given tactics to use during your internship to help you get the most out of the experience (Chapter 10). The final chapter (11) provides an honest conversation about what to expect upon graduation, walking you through the first days, months, and year after graduation.

Teaching and sharing my knowledge and experiences is my passion. I want to see every student be successful. I wrote this book as a roadmap for you to use. Make the most of your college journey by creating experiences you will be excited to talk about with prospective employers. Keep elevating your collection of skills and experiences.

Cheers!
Diane M. Monahan, PhD

Part I

YOU ARE THE KEY TO YOUR OWN SUCCESS

CHAPTER 1

It's Never Too Early to Think About Your Career

One of the biggest decisions you've made is selecting a college. Your story might have gone something like this: You started by exploring university websites, visiting campuses, and completing applications. One spring day you received responses from the universities you were waiting to hear from. You sat by the computer waiting for updates on the status of your application and discussed your options with your family and friends. You ran numbers comparing financial obligations and thought about the opportunities of each location. You wrote down a list of pros and cons, hoping the answer would reveal itself to you. And it did! Fast forward to the fall, with bags packed and shower shoes tucked in a box, you arrived on campus, your home for the next four years, welcomed by all the fanfare of move-in day. Your story may vary some from this, but you applied to a college, were accepted, and started your journey to earn a degree in communication. The journey you are on is an exciting one made up of opportunities and countless experiences. As we'll discuss throughout this book, don't wait to be prepared. Don't wait for a single piece of paper to change your life at graduation; invest in all the learning experiences that support and lift up your diploma.

Deciding to attend college and selecting the right fit took time and effort. Members of your family and school probably guided you to resources to help you make your decision. Now as you are walking around campus, grasping your smartphone displaying you class schedule, you may be wondering what the introduction to philosophy class has to do with your intended career in communication. It is easy to become disconnected with your career goals during the first two years of college. The average undergraduate student takes 40 classes in their bachelor studies, of which as few as 10 to 12 courses are major specific. For many this is a disappointing revelation in the first year. It is common to feel underwhelmed while completing required general education courses; after all, it was likely your major that inspired you to go to college, and it is normal to be most excited about taking classes directly related to your future career. It is a misnomer that career preparation takes place in your senior year. Earl Nightingale, an American radio speaker and author, once said, "People with goals succeed because they know where they're going" (2020). It is never too early to think about your career. It is to your advantage to use all four years of your bachelor degree to gain experiences and skills. After all it is these experiences and skills that will be the substance of your stories and interview responses. The information that fills the pages of this book serves as tool to guide you in your career journey, starting your freshman year. It is valuable to embark on a journey of self-discovery

The chapters of this book are designed and organized in a way that leads you through your career-focused journey, using your degree in communication. Your journey begins with gaining a better understand of the often-dreaded general education courses and how they can be used to gain experience, pieces for your portfolio, and the like. Recognizing the value in general education courses can prepare you for the communication major and pave the path for job opportunities. The best approach to your college experience is to see opportunities in all that you are exposed to and determine how they relate to your passions. Later in the book we will discuss capitalizing on your strengths and diminishing your weaknesses. Embracing all of your current learning experiences, connecting with others to help you through the process, and being an active agent in your growth and development is the ultimate goal of this book. The journey toward your future career is a worthwhile one.

The Reason for General Education Requirements

A good starting place gaining an understanding of why universities and colleges require a common core of courses referred to as **general education** requirements. A bachelor's degree requires a minimum number of semester or quarter credits. This number varies across universities and programs (majors); however, a common requirement is 120 semester credits. The credits are distributed across three main categories: general education, major, and electives or minor. Most core curriculum, the general education requirements, consist of one or two courses in each of the major disciplines: English; history; science; mathematics; health/fitness; and maybe

religion, culture, and a foreign language (see Figure 1.1). In your freshman year you may have enrolled in a first-year experience or freshman seminar. Universities use this type of course to help assimilate first-time college students into the university culture and provide support during this time of transition. In addition to preparing students for a specific profession, one of the intended goals of college education is helping students become informed about the world in which they live. It is easy to reduce the goal of general education to helping students become well rounded, but this is shortchanging the many benefits of the general education curriculum.

General education requirements are more important than you may first think. The general education core provides a necessary foundation for critical thinking and transferable skills necessary for being successful in college, one's profession, and life. A child is first socialized by their family. This process continues

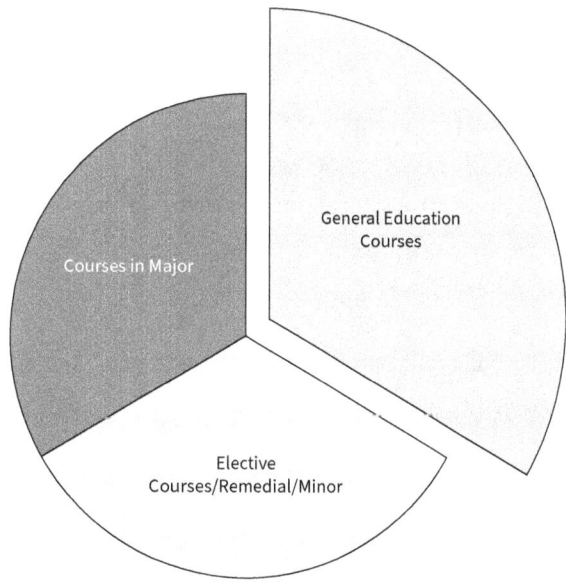

FIGURE 1.1 Categories of Courses

more profoundly in elementary and secondary school. Sociologists refer to the things and people that influence one's development as "agents" (Cole, 2019). There are six influencers commonly considered to be agents: family, school, peers, mass media, technology, and work. It is believed that one's family is the first agent that helps set values, form basic attitudes, and contribute to one's self-image and identity. This process continues when a child enters school, which informs their discipline, order, cooperation, and conformity. It is with peers that a person learns to deal with conflict, competition, and empathy. The ever-present mass media emphasizes and challenges norms and provides role models—positive and negative—for people to imitate. Work, as a socialization agent, emphasizes assimilating to organizational culture, responsibility, and productivity. Higher education plays an important role in one's socialization by helping students translate academic study into knowledge, discipline, and responsibility across several areas beyond one's career field. The ability to translate and apply skills learned in one class to different classes is a skill that will benefit you in your career. Don't overlook the value of learning general skills, such as problem-solving, effective communication, analyzing information, and thinking independently. These skills are often referred to as **power skills**.

Approaches to general education curriculum fall into three categories: distributive, integrative, and hybrid. A distributive program is one that requires students to take a specific number of courses in each major discipline. It generally does not allow for much flexibility or options. Does your university require you to take two sciences courses from a predetermined list? If so, it is likely your university ascribes to the distribution approach. Other universities take more of integrative approach to general education. This approach focuses not so much on specific content or courses but skill acquisition and skill transfer. If your university requires you to take a sequence of courses that share skill building, it is likely your university uses the integrative approach. The third type is a hybrid model, blending both the distribution approach and integrative approach. According to Hart (2015), about half of universities in the United States employ the hybrid model.

Finding the Competitive Advantage in General Education

Now that you better understand the general education core, let's turn our attention to finding the competitive advantage of these courses. How do these requirements prepare you for your intended career? When preparing for the job market it is important

for you to present yourself as the superior choice over other applicants. Maximizing opportunities to learn something new and understand how it benefits you and your future career is a key to success.

There are several advantages to fulfilling the requirements of general education. The courses you will take in the general education program will help you build a base of knowledge, and this knowledge will be useful as you begin to develop your career. For example, the information you gain in your history class will help you navigate conversations of politics during a business networking event or dinner. Also, history helps you hone your skills in understanding contexts and analyzing problems and solutions. For those interested in public relations, history is a great resource of lessons learned. Did you know the field of public relations dates back to before the American Revolutionary War? Challenge yourself to process the information presented in your classes in a manner that allows you to gain insight into varying perspectives. The general education core also provides an opportunity to gain an understanding of the world around you, including fields other than your own. As you take your general education courses, consider your interest level and how the course connects to your communication major. You might be surprised how a general education course might spark interest in a double major, minor, or specific career focus.

SPOTLIGHT ON COMMUNICATION
Cognitive Scripts

Our brains process information and store it in cognitive "files." These files allow us to access information when we need it. The more we do something the more embedded the information is creating a **cognitive script** (Meng, 2008). Like in the movies, scripts guide our behavior and communication in a specific context. Have you ever noticed that you have a script for buying groceries? You likely engage in conversation with the clerk almost effortlessly. The more exposure you have to different pieces of information and experiences the more cognitive scripts you will have for future use. Our scripts are informed by our environment and experiences. Scripts are unique to each person but are considered resistant to change. Remember that time you responded to the clerk by saying, "You too!" when the clerk wished you well on your upcoming vacation. You expected the routine interaction to end with, "Have a nice day." You relied on your script for interacting with the clerk. Putting the science aside, it makes sense that the more options you have for approaching situations and problems the greater chance you have of being successful.

What do cognitive scripts have to do with getting your dream job after college? According to Meng (2008), cognitive scripts are contextual and often known as social scripts. There are several components required to creating such a script. One component is the event frame, which refers to context of the location the event occurs. The second component of scripts are the social roles present in the event. Social roles of the participants are key to creating scripts. Episodic function is the third component of creating scripts. Think about how interactions are made up of scenes or episodes very similar to your favorite television series or movie. Meng asserts that people internalize information that each of the components provide to make sense of the information. This sense-making results in the creation of scripts. When you are attending the classes for your general education requirements you are processing hundreds of events, all containing information of the three components. Employees across fields are often called upon to make decisions quickly. Having more well-formed scripts at your disposal will increase your options for responding. Remember that scripts are a type of shorthand your brain makes when processing information. It is to your benefit to take advantage of every opportunity to build a depository of scripts.

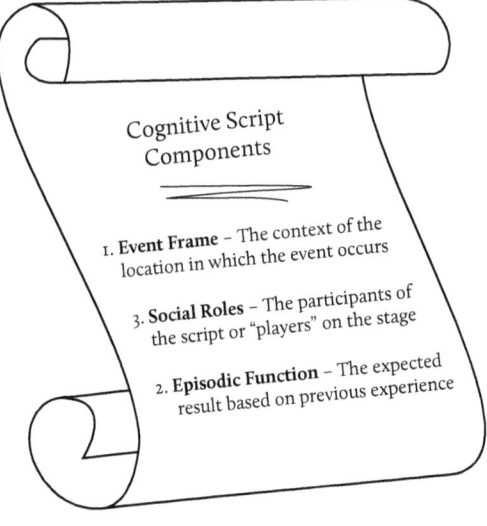

Cognitive Script Components

1. **Event Frame** – The context of the location in which the event occurs
3. **Social Roles** – The participants of the script or "players" on the stage
2. **Episodic Function** – The expected result based on previous experience

IMG 1.3

> **EXERCISE 1.1**
> **Building a Base of Knowledge**
>
> Consider three general education courses you are enrolled in currently or have completed in a previous semester. Write the name of the course and one thing you learned in that course. In the two right columns write two ways you could apply this knowledge in future classes, interviews, in the workplace, and so on. It is recommended that you add to the list throughout your college careers. Try keeping a "knowledge and application" journal throughout your college years. Use the journal to capture how you could use what you have learned to see issues and problems from different perspectives.
>
> | | Course | Knowledge | Application 1 | Application 2 |
> |---|---|---|---|---|
> | 1 | | | | |
> | 2 | | | | |
> | 3 | | | | |

A second advantage to the general education program is enhancing your communication skills. One of the key competencies for communication majors is effective messaging. Being able to practice creating messages, both written and oral, provides opportunities to strengthen weaknesses and build on strengthens. As a communication major it is invaluable to have experience writing and presenting on topics that might not be a true interest. Prospective employers will see a major in communication as a testament of strong verbal communication skills. Communication majors often take on oral and written communication tasks in the workplace. For example, public relations practitioners are required to be skilled across five essential abilities: research, writing, planning, problem-solving, and business. Some of your best work may be great portfolio pieces. There are many important communication skills you should master before graduating college. Listening, public speaking, networking, working in groups, and giving and receiving feedback are just a few competencies that are key to professional success. General education classes will expose you to instructors that do not teach classes in your major. All instructors are links in your professional network. In the future, you might want to ask one of the instructors to write a letter of reference for an internship, job, or graduate school. General education classes are filled with students representing many different majors. It is likely that in your junior and senior years you will be taking classes with many of the same students in you major. In your general education classes, you will meet students from all majors which will strengthen your listening skills as well as require you to work in groups. Through class discussion or conversation, you will learn about your classmates. Your classmates will add to your personal and professional network. The person sitting next to you might have a family member who is the hiring agent for the public relations firm you are dreaming about interning for. College presents an ideal environment for meeting with all types of people from different backgrounds.

A third benefit of general education courses is that they improve your critical thinking skills. Critical thinking requires you to create, evaluate, analyze, apply, understand, and remember. In your general education courses you should develop a questioning mind and form a habit of asking meaningful questions. This skill will transfer to your career in communication. To create effective messages, you must understand the context of the message. Use the opportunities presented by class discussions to ask questions that help you connect the material to something you are curious about or your future career. A great tool to utilize in your classes is thinking about the material in terms of three types of questions:

- **Comprehension questions** seek further explanation to help you understand the material. This is the most common type of questions students ask in class. When you are seeking clarity about something you ask for more information. It is a great habit to engage your faculty during class by answering and asking comprehension questions. After all, you are paying for the classes, so be sure you are getting everything you can from the experience of each course.

- **Connecting questions** help you link the information with something you previously learned or to another class. As an instructor, I like when students connect what I am teaching with something else they have learned, especially in another class. A connecting question represents the spirit of higher education. Throughout your college years you will be making connections with all that you encounter—people, places, and information.

- **Bridge questions** are similar to connecting questions, except the information is being connected to something outside of the classroom. Ideally, a bridging question takes what you are learning in the class and applies it to the "real world." Use a bridge to better understand the world around you, including your intended career. Bridge questions represent critical thinking.

Whether you are in a general education course or a communication course, you should strive to make connections between what you are learning and what you are experiencing in the world around you. This might be the most important type of question you should be asking to further your career preparation. All three types of questions will enrich your learning experiences and help you practice independent thinking, which is an invaluable skill. You will practice asking meaningful questions in exercise 1.2.

EXERCISE 1.2
Creating a Habit of Asking Meaningful Questions

Think of a specific class you recently attended. In the following space, write a brief description of the material discussed in class. In the following table, write two questions you could ask in class for each type of question.

Discuss the class topic:

_____

_____

_____

Comprehension	Connecting	Bridge
1.	1.	1.
2.	2.	2.

The **competitive advantage** of general education courses is that they can help with your career. As previously discussed, if you approach your general education courses strategically you will profit from gaining transferable skills. Hiring agents state that employers are require employees to use a broader set of skills and take on more responsibility (Bradford, 2018). The information age and technology age has made information more readily available but at the same time more complex. Employers desire employees who know more than basic skills and can demonstrate higher-order thinking. Stepping outside your comfort zone is a key to your success. A general education curriculum can help you become well versed in multiple subjects. You will become better at independent and critical thinking, dealing with unforeseen issues, and solving problems. These classes provide an overlooked benefit of self-discovery. Self-discovery is built into the college curriculum, allowing you to explore other fields without getting off track or wasting semester credits.

In summary, the general education curriculum helps you (1) acquire broad knowledge, (2) gain intellectual and real-world skills, (3) understand cultural differences and engage with others, (4) evaluate ethical consequences, and (5) make connections across academic courses. Embrace the general education core and where it takes you on your career journey.

The Role of the Academic Advisor

This chapter has presented reasons why it is never too early to think about your career. Even the prescribed general education requirements present hidden opportunities to develop workplace skills. Waiting until your senior year to develop a strategy for entering the job market is a grave mistake. Upon entering college, you will be assigned an academic advisor. The structure of academic advising varies across universities, but it is common to be assigned a success coach or general advisor as a freshman and then be reassigned to a faculty member who serves as your academic advisor in later semesters. Your university may assign freshmen to academic advisors in the first semester. Your advisor is usually responsible for tracking your progress toward degree completion, assisting you with selecting and registering for classes, helping you understand university policies and procedures, and signing required forms. Additionally, your advisor is an expert in your major. It is important that you establish a relationship with your advisor. Your academic advisor has an established network within the university and your intended profession. This person is a great resource for being connected with other faculty and staff that can assist you when they cannot. They can connect you with established professionals, who could potentially serve as a mentor provide valuable internship opportunities. Your academic advisor can provide advice about class load or sequencing as well as your career path, and they will expect you to initiate contact. Some first-year seminars or freshman experiences require you to meet with your advisor and have a preliminary conservation. Regardless, you should contact your academic advisor early and regularly.

SPOTLIGHT ON COMMUNICATION
Mentoring

There are many different types of **mentoring r**elationships, ranging from informal to formal, face-to-face to virtual, and peer to professional. Informal mentorships are relationships without written agreements or established meeting times. While not all academic advisors serve as a mentor, many can be informal mentors. Formal mentorships usually have written agreements, established meeting times, and ongoing involvement. Ongoing involvement can be frequent (e.g., daily) or less frequent (e.g., monthly). Face-to-face mentors will be in the same location as their mentees. In college you usually meet with your advisor face to face, although after graduation you may continue the mentorship virtually. Virtual mentors are not physically present, and interactions take place through written communication or phone calls. Peer mentors share the same level of experience and knowledge, whereas professional mentors often hold aspirational positions in your target profession.

You have responsibilities as a mentee. It is important that you take charge of your own development, as staying focused on your goals will only benefit you. Don't wait for your mentor to ask for meetings. Be organized and preplan meetings. Inform your mentor of the agenda in advance of meetings. Use the meetings as an opportunity to gain needed information and advice; seek feedback on your career plan. Keep in touch with your mentor and update them as you implement recommendations.

TABLE 1.1

Attributes of a Mentee	Attributes of a Mentor
Planner	Guide
Communicator	Teacher
Driver	Advisor
Learner	Motivator

In summary, it is important for you to write down your intended profession and keep it visible, starting your freshman year. Keep in the forefront of your mind and actions the reason you are attending college. Understand that valuable opportunities are often in disguise. Opportunities may be found in the "must take" general education courses. The course furthest from your intended communication may present excellent networking or a context in which to practice the communication profession. For most, there is not an employer waiting for you to complete your degree. Rather, you have to create opportunities for yourself. Recognizing the chance to gain experiences and skills early on will set you apart from your peers. I invited a guest speaker to present to my department's chapter of the National Communication

Association's honor society: Lambda Pi Eta. The guest held the position of director of regional communication for a well-known national fast food chain. The young professional was not many years from her own college graduation. Students were interested in the story of her career and wondered how she got such great job after graduation. They asked if she had a high-profile internship. She said no. They asked if she held a full-time job with the company while she was a student. She said no. Finally, she revealed the secret of her early success. She explained that in her public relations class she had to create a press kit for a business. She used the feedback from her instructor to improve her press kit and added it to her portfolio. The guest speaker described how she was able to use portfolio pieces from many noncommunication courses to strengthen her application. This professional represented how much you are the key to your success. Chapter 2 will discuss how to create a pathway to having the first job of your career in communication upon graduation. The chapter presents how understanding your values, interests, and skills provides valuable insight into your career path.

TOOLS FOR THINKING ABOUT YOUR CAREER EARLY

Here is a list of resources to watch and read. Each reinforces the topics presented in the chapter.

Matt Cutts (2011): "Something New For 30 Days"

Matt Cutts challenges you to think of something you want to do and do it for 30 days. He speaks about how these 30-day challenges changed his life. Small sustainable changes are easier to achieve and can lead to bigger changes. Creating habits that will impact your college experience and your future career is important.

WATCH AT https://www.youtube.com/watch?v=JnfBXjWm7hc

Margaret Heffernan (2012): "Dare to Disagree"

Margaret Heffernan discusses the importance of asking questions and seeking answers to problems. In this brief TED Talk, Heffernan recommends avoiding sheepishly going through your college experiences. Instead, seek ways to be an active agent. Embrace different ways

(continued ...)

of thinking. Seek out people who are different from you, and engage with them. Your college years might not go as planned, but remember each experience can result in something positive: growth.

WATCH AT https://www.youtube.com/watch?v=PY_kd46RfVE

Emilie Wapnick (2015): "Why Some of Us Don't Have One True Calling"

Emilie Wapnick emphasizes that you should not be stressed if you do not know exactly what you want to do upon graduation. She introduces the concept of "multipotentialites." She uses this term to describe people who have a range of interests and jobs over a lifetime.

WATCH AT https://www.youtube.com/watch?v=4sZdcB6bjI8

Citizen Bank (n.d): "10 College Life Hacks Every Freshman Should Know"

This brief article presents a list of 10 suggestions for adjusting and thriving in college. Consider what advice you would give other students. Perhaps consider writing a blog post for your university's social media or an article for your campus newspaper.

READ AT https://www.citizensbank.com/learning/10-things-every-college-freshman-should-know.aspx

Greg Shirley (2018): "You're Always On: Your Career Development Cycle"

Dr. Greg Shirley shares advice for career development. He discusses the career development cycle and why it is a process of always revisiting your growth and development. He then offers specific steps with examples.

(continued ...)

WATCH AT https://www.ted.com/talks/greg_shirley_you_re_always_on_your_career_development_cycle

Michelle Fox (2020): "Here's How the Pandemic is Reshaping Career Planning for College Students"

In this article, Michelle Fox discusses how career planning has been impacted by the pandemic. As a college student, these are unique times. Use this article to learn how career development has changed. Knowing this information will help you better prepare for your specific career. The information in the article can be helpful when interviewing for internships and jobs.

READ AT https://www.cnbc.com/2020/06/11/how-the-pandemic-is-reshaping-career-planning-for-college-students.html

KEY TERMS

bridge questions: Questions that are similar to connecting questions except the information is being connected to something outside of the classroom.

cognitive script: Our brains process information and stores it in cognitive files. These files allow us to access information when we need it. A script is a stored memory of how we communicated or performed a previous task. The more often you complete the task the more solid the script becomes and is used repeatedly.

competitive advantage: Skills, attributes, and experiences that distinguishes you from your competitors, such as other applicants, students and employees.

comprehension questions: A question that seeks further explanation to help you understand the material. This is the most common type of questions that students ask in class. When you are seeking clarity about something you ask for more information.

connecting questions: A question that helps you link the information with something you previously learned or to another class.

general education: A common core of courses required by universities to earn a bachelor degree. Usually the general education core consists of core subjects like English; history; science; mathematics; health/fitness; and religion, culture, and a foreign language.

mentoring: A professional relationship where one person has more experience and coaches the another person to gain more of a competitive advantage in the field or job market.

power skills: General skills, such as problem solving, effective communication, analyzing information and thinking independently, that are basic skills necessary for job success. Power skills are not discipline-specific skills.

CREDITS

IMG 1.1: Copyright © 2020 Pexels/Andrea Piacquadio.
IMG 1.2: Copyright © 2020 Unsplash/GR Stocks.
IMG 1.3: Copyright © 2022 Pixabay/Clker-Free-Vector-Images.

CHAPTER 2

Identifying Your Values, Interests, and Skills

When you started college, you were probably equally excited and confused. When you watch your peers in class it may be clear to you that some are laser focused on their targeted careers, though you may feel anything but certain of your future career when you look in the mirror you. Rather, it's possible you see uncertainty looking back at you. I assure you that most undergraduate students are just as uncertain about what their future career holds for them. Some people are better at masking their uncertainty; others have learned skills helpful for self-discovery. According to the United States Department of Education (2017), it is common for undergraduate students pursuing associate's or bachelor's degrees to change their majors within the first three years of study. Many students enter college having no idea what to study or career path to take. Ohio State University (n.d.) states as many as 75% of students change their major at least once before graduating. Uncertainty is a normal part of being a college student, and your college years are a great time of exploration, reflection, and education. Aristotle is credited as saying, "Knowing yourself is the beginning of all wisdom." In this chapter, we explore the three elements of knowing yourself that form the foundation of your career choice. Values, interests, and skills should provide a path to career discovery.

The idea of thinking about a lifelong career at the start of your college journey may be daunting or even almost debilitating. You often hear that college is the best years of your life, yet you have the looming awareness that you need to be prepared to be "launched" into real life upon graduation. With one symbolic move of the tassel from left to right, you are supposed to be ready to start on the path to a fulfilling career. The truth is that you began the path the day you stepped onto campus. The purpose of this chapter is to present a GPS of sorts to help you navigate through the different forks in the road leading to your destination upon graduation. Three valuable components of career success, values, interests, and skills, can be used to make your journey more fulfilling and even a bit more certain. By the end of the chapter, you should know more about your professional profile. This profile should help provide the foundation for translating your college experiences into workplace-ready experiences. These experiences will be disguised as opportunities you encounter both inside and outside of the classroom. The GPS will help you navigate through the many opportunities and choose the best path to reach your desired career. The chapter concludes with specific tools to guide you through making the best decisions and choices for you and your future career.

In a time of sophisticated technology, wouldn't it be wonderful to think that a contraption could chart the course for you as you embark on your career as simply as requesting directions from your GPS to the local restaurant? Input some information, and poof! The result is your specific career. Clear. Defined. Charted. But it doesn't exactly work that way. Why is so much thought, planning, and work needed to be successful? The fact is there is not as much mystery in identifying a career as you might think. It is important to acknowledge that you will need to play an active role in your career readiness. Creating a pathway to a career upon graduation begins with first understanding who you are. In *Alice in Wonderland*, Lewis Carroll (2018) wrote, "Who in the world am I? Ah, that's the great puzzle." Your pathway is not being created from nothing; instead, the life you have lived plays a role. What you believe to be important in life plays a role. You already know what you like and what you dislike. Dusting off the uncertainty, you will find your values, interests, and skills.

I have often described career preparation to my students as an art closet. Imagine having a large room filled with every imaginable art supply. Consider you and other students are tasked with spending 3 hours in the room and creating a model of a structure in which to live. How would you approach this task? What is the very first thing you do? What items would you reach for? Would it be the large piece of white poster board, the empty wrapping paper tube, or even the stack of Popsicle sticks? Would you use lots of glue, or is glue too messy for you; instead, would you grab the double-sided tape? Are you the person who would stand back and take inventory of the options, or would you jump right in? In my experience students approach this activity in two different ways. The first group skips the preparation stage because they are in a rush to see the finished product. After all, who doesn't like to be finished and to admire all their work? The second group loses track of time, and hours go by as they explore different options, not afraid of failure or mistakes. Understanding how you approach "work" and learning is the underlying factor that forms your approach, which is valuable for moving toward developing a pathway to your career. In the next sections, I will show how understanding your values, interests, and skills plays an essential role in developing an actionable plan to reaching a career upon graduation.

Values Guide Your Future Career

A common definition of **values** is a set of principles or standards that guides a person's behaviors. Values are judgments of what is important to a person, and they influence how one lives and works. Think of values as the ruler you measure things against. How something measures up probably determines how you integrate it into your life or work. In short, values are measures you use to determine if life is turning out the way you want it to. Scott Jeffrey (n.d.) wrote a guide on personal values. In it he states, "Values aren't selected; they're discovered. We don't choose our values. Our values reveal themselves to us." Values determine how you behave and make decisions. Following, I describe values and the two specific types of values.

"Values" is an umbrella term, consisting of specific subtypes, including **core** and **broad values**. Core values, furthermore, are often categorized into three types. The three types of core values include intrinsic values, extrinsic values, and lifestyle values:

- **Intrinsic values:** Intrinsic values refer to what motivates you internally to do what you do, such as work. When applying core values to your future career, intrinsic values motivate you do the work you do. If you career aligns with your intrinsic values, then you have a sense of being fulfilled by your career. An example of this is working for a nonprofit organization doing public relations, rather than a corporate one, because the nature of your job is more important to you than the salary. Nationally, the average salary of a public relations practitioner at a nonprofit is approximately $54,000, whereas the corporate counterpart's average salary is approximately $80,000. Intrinsic values can also include things like having ample variety in work tasks, opportunities to take risks, or building a respected presence for yourself. If you are a person motivated by doing good and you subscribe to the nonprofit mission of serving others and not driven by money, then your intrinsic values align with the work you are doing at the nonprofit.

- **Extrinsic values:** Extrinsic values refer to tangible rewards you receive from your career. The most common example of extrinsic rewards you receive from work is money or pay. However, there are other extrinsic rewards to be gained from your career, such as gaining the ability to influence, recognition, job security, travel, a flexible work schedule, autonomy, and being part of a team. The work environment can be an important source of extrinsic value.

- **Lifestyle values:** Lifestyle values refer to how you want to live. These values determine your lifestyle. Do you want to live in a big city or internationally? Do you imagine your work taking you to far and distant lands? Would you move away from friends and family to pursue your dream job?

EXERCISE 2.1
Assessing Your Core Values

Review the following list of values. Rank (with 1 being the most important, 2 being the second most important, and so on) each one in terms of importance to you. After ranking the values, use the information following the table to interpret the results.

A. Taking risks	I. Helping others	Q. Living internationally
B. Working to better my community	J. Living in a big city	R. Having a big salary
C. Having my work recognized	K. Feeling respected at work	S. Having variety and change at work
D. Traveling for work	L. Saving money	T. Owning a home
E. Spending time with friends and family	M. Having a flexible work schedule	U. Having vacation time
F. Having autonomy	N. Having a sense of accomplishment	V. Being productive
G. Being famous or well known	O. Being creative	W. Having a set structure
H. Having cooperative colleagues	P. Enjoying my work	X. Owning a second home

Look at the values you scored the highest. It will be important to you to find a career that aligns with the top values from your assessment. For further insight, group the values according to their type:

- **Intrinsic values:** A, B, C, H, I, K, N, O, P, S
- **Extrinsic values:** D, F, G, Q, R, V, W
- **Lifestyle values:** E, J, L, T, U, X

In each category, examine how you ranked the values listed. You may see a pattern of what type of values motivates you the most in the workplace.

In is worth mentioning that personal core values provide the foundational beliefs that dictate your behavior. Broad values are often called "personal values," and these values usually transfer across specific contexts. Writers often identify five primary values that transfer across contexts: integrity, accountability, diligence, perseverance, and discipline. Figure 2.1 shows a visual of the five values. Examples of noncore values may include compassion, creativity, and connection. Personal values will influence your core values in the workplace.

Your purpose in life is determined by the type of impact you want to make in the world around you as well as how you want to live.

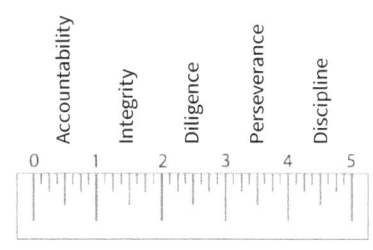

FIGURE 2.1 Example of Values: A Ruler for Life

There are many ways to examine your core values and personal set of values. In addition to the exercise you just completed you may want to examine how the values you ranked high are personified in the people you most admire. I recommend reading about the professionals that lead the field you are considering as a career. For example, if you are interested in public relations, visit the Public Relations Society of America website (www.prsa.org). There is a vast amount of information available about the profession and resources for undergraduate students. The Public Relations Society of America also has a useful student chapter. If you are a future broadcaster, visit the National Association of Broadcasters' website (https://www.nab.org). The National Association of Crisis Organization Directors (https://www.nascod.org/) provides resources and support for directors of crisis service centers. There are several other associations for communication professionals, such as the National Communication Association, the International Association of Business Communicators, the IEEE Professional Communication Society, and the Association for Women in Communications. Being more familiar with professional organizations will provide you with information regarding different professions. The best way to find additional resources on professional organizations is to ask your faculty. Faculty are very familiar with professional associations and, after, often become members themselves. You can also search the internet for professional associations in your specific field of interest.

The next step to understanding how your values influence your future career choice is putting it together with how you envision values aligning with your future career. In Exercise 2.2, write a paragraph describing how you see your top ranked values from Exercise 2.1 aligning with your career. Describe what you will be doing, how the work will be done, why you want to do this work, and where you will be doing this work. You should see in your completed description a reflection of the intrinsic, extrinsic, and lifestyle values that are important to you.

EXERCISE 2.2
Your Work Values Story

Write a paragraph describing how you see your top five values in your future career:

_____
_____
_____
_____
_____
_____
_____
_____
_____

Interests Add Color to Your Work

Phil Hansen, an artist, has a 2013 TED Talk that is very impactful when thinking about a career path. He speaks about his passion for art and desire to make it a career. As a young man, he developed a shake in his hands, but he pressed on with his art, until it became depilating—or so he thought. He made an appointment with a neurologist, who told him to "embrace the shake" and use it to his advantage in creating his art. The lesson is sometimes you have to look past how you perceive things to be and challenge yourself to adopt another perspective, or even multiple perspectives. Hansen did just that, and he come up with novel directives for creating art. He made inspiring pieces of art using burger grease, paper cups, candles, fire, and so many other items. He reimagined how his passion for art could be realized.

Confucius is often attributed as saying, "Choose a job you love, and you will never have to work a day in your life." This sentiment suggests that our interests should drive our career choice. One can assume by your choice of communication as you undergraduate major that you have a deep interest in some aspect of communication. Maybe you enjoy interpersonal communication, organizational communication, or mass communication. Maybe you are not sure and are hoping to discover your passion through your time at college. Communication is ranked as the second most popular major in the nation, according to *Princeton Review* in 2022. Communication, like psychology, is often a solid choice of major because it demonstrates to potential employers that, at the very least, you have an interest in understanding the creation of a message for a target audience. This is important at some level in most professions. Your **interests** are the things you like to do. Many students I have taught over the years tell me they want to work in public relations. When I ask why, they tell me how much of a people person they are and how they hate to write. The reality is that public relations practitioners spend upwards of 80% of their job writing. If you don't have an interest in writing, a public relations career will not align with your interests. If talking and interacting with people is what excites you, you will need to find a career that best capitalizes on these interests. It is important to find out as much as possible about your desired career to ensure it aligns with your interests. In your quest for information, you may discover that it is not public relations that excites you but marketing or event planning.

There are many things that shape our interests. Think about what you enjoy. Do you have hobbies or special talents? Do you like to dance? Or maybe you enjoy horseback riding. The main influencers shaping our interests include the following: the different roles we play, our work experience, our cultural background, our economic and social conditions, our personalities, and our families. Through the socialization process children are exposed to different experiences. It is this process that helps us realize what we like and don't like to do. Think back to when you were a child. Did you enjoy cleaning up your room? Did you spend hours organizing? Although it might seem simplistic, whether you cleaned up you room may influence your future career choice. This activity may be related to your skill of organizing, which could be connected to a career in event planning.

There are tools to help you identify your interests and understand how they potentially connect to your future career. An interest inventory is the most common way of self-identifying your interests. Such inventories will measure your interests across different categories, including leisure activities, work tasks, the type of people you prefer to work with, and topics you like.

EXERCISE 2.3
Identifying Your Interests

The following interest inventory has been adapted from Tufts University's Career Center (n.d.). Think about your free time. What do you most enjoy doing? Circle each item you enjoy. It is helpful to go through the list a second time and mark off the things you could not see yourself doing for an extended period. In other words, mark off the things you enjoy but know you would become bored or disinterested of if you had to do them every day. Now, review the list of patterns. Do the items you selected share something in common? If so, what? Through this activity you should have a better idea of what types of things interest you and what do not. Consider how you could make a career out of what interests you.

- Creating new things
- Learning how things work
- Philosophy
- Dissecting an organism
- Engaging in business
- Playing team sports
- Selling things
- Analyzing systems
- Solving crossword puzzles
- Public speaking
- Teaching others
- Graphic design
- Being around animals
- Scientific research
- Studying the media
- Reading
- Analyzing movies
- Designing things
- Caring for the sick
- Meeting people
- Rearranging furniture
- Decorating things
- Collecting things
- Studying artifacts
- Studying maps
- Data processing
- Observing human behavior
- Analytical writing
- Debating
- Using social media tools
- Supervising people
- Video games
- Dancing
- Ballet
- Birdwatching
- Anticipating others' needs
- Visiting the elderly
- Socializing
- Joining public causes
- Talking about politics
- Studying art
- Organizing information/records
- Working with animals
- Studying stocks/investments
- Writing poetry and stories
- Science fiction
- Studying languages
- Church activities
- Exploring new places
- Resolving conflicts
- Photography
- Listening to music
- Traveling
- Playing with children
- Solving problems
- Working with numbers
- Charity work
- Budgeting
- Giving advice
- Planning events

John Holland's **RIASEC theory** is the most widely accepted theory about how individuals make career choices (Kennelly et al., 2018). In the late 90s, Holland explained that people develop their own personal career theory regarding beliefs, ideas, and even assumptions about careers and types of work. This personal career theory influences an individual's career choice. According to Holland (1997), this explains why you decide to persist and why you change your mind regarding career choice. According to Holland, you encounter uncertainty in choosing a career when personal characteristics are not aligned with the nature of the chosen career. Also, a lack of knowledge about the career's expectations, duties, and responsibilities can influence your happiness in a particular career. Lastly, Holland argues that if you don't have the required skills required for the chosen career you are faced with either putting more intensive effort in to catch up or changing your mind. For example, it is common on campuses across the nation for students to start out premedicine, preveterinarian, or prelaw. After the first semester or two, students often realize they are being challenged by the science and math courses. Usually at this point, students reflect on what they are willing to do to continue in the program and self-assess their aptitude for the subject matter. The result is many students change their mind and, hence, change their major. Communication and other fields often receive some of these students. The assessments throughout this chapter and book will help you learn more about your personal career theory.

Holland identified six job personality and work environment types. The six types include realistic, investigative, artistic, social, enterprising, and conventional. He argues that most individuals are one of the six types. People look for careers in which they can be around others who are like minded. It is easier to assimilate into a new work environment made up of people with similar approaches to work. In addition, people look for work environments that allow them to make the most of their skills, abilities, knowledge, and values. Holland believes that finding a work environment that best aligns with your personality and approach to work will result in enjoyment and career satisfaction. It makes sense that your behavior is connected to your personality and the environment you are working in (and living in, for that matter). Let's review each of the six job personality and work environment types in the following sections.

Realistic

People in the **realistic** category are known as "doers." If you are realistic person you likely prefer physical activities requiring skills, strength, and often coordination.

You probably enjoy the outdoors and working with your hands. Realistic individuals like fixing, assembling, and building things. They are also good at using and operating equipment, tools, and machines. Common personality traits shared by realistic people include genuineness, stability, conformity, and practicality. You may be wondering what type of careers realistic people are best suited for. Often, these people find their way to careers in technology, computing, business, agriculture, horticulture, and the armed services. The natural next question you may be thinking is, "Now what? How do I use my communication degree to get a job to match my personality and work environment type?" Don't be dismayed. There are many careers in the communication field that need realistic types of employees. Keep in mind that communication is a very broad field. This is likely one of the reasons you choose it as a major! If you fall in this category you may want to consider the following careers: public relations on a military base, video producer, music/sound engineer, emergency communication, aviation communication, park superintendent, concert stage engineer, lighting engineer, front-of-the-house engineer, and event staging audio engineer—just to name a new. I once had a student who loved skateboarding. She did it competitively. Once, we had a discussion of her future career goals. I told her you if love skateboarding, then find a career that keeps you connected to it. She ended up doing two internships with a local skateboarding facility. Upon graduation, she was hired as the company's social media expert. It was the best of both worlds. I had another student who did an internship with the roller derby and was able to combine his interest in the roller derby and communication. The best advice is to find an interest and do your research on all the different types of jobs associated with that interest.

Investigative

People in the **investigative** category are known as "thinkers." If you are an investigative person you like to observe, learn, analyze, evaluate, and problem-solve. You probably prefer to work with theory and information. Common personality traits shared by investigative people include being analytical, curious, and independent. If you are investigative you are good at communicating by writing and speaking. You may also enjoy using technology to design. This category is a natural fit for many careers in communication. For example, you may desire to continue to graduate school with an eye on becoming a university professor. Many reporters, especially investigative reporters, are investigative personalities. You may also consider a career in law. Communication is among the most popular majors of students entering law school. I had a student who received his undergraduate degree in communication and graduate degree in communication advocacy before entering law school. He is now a practicing lawyer. Other careers that would align with this personality group are research positions at a think tank, social media analyst, and careers in criminal justice.

Artistic

People in the **artistic** category are known as "creators." If you are an artistic person you like to use words, art, music, or drama to communicate and express yourself. Artistic individuals enjoy being creative and original. Often, artistic people are unsystematic in their processes and activities.

Common personality traits shared by artistic people include being imaginative, disorderly, idealistic, emotional, and sometimes impractical. One distinguishing characteristic is being a dreamer. Some examples of aligning professions include artist, musician, and writer. There are many communication careers well-matched for you if you are an artistic personality type, including the following: graphic artist, illustrator, photographer, sign writer, composer, actor, reporter, writer, editor, advertiser, and fashion designer—just to name a few. I had a student who exceled in drawing and was able to transfer that skill and interest to a career as a graphic artist. I also had a student who was a singer and loved music. She thought the natural career with her degree in communication was public relations, but she ended up in radio. Many artistic people find their way to a career in public relations. Social media writer and manager is another great career that aligns with the artistic personality type.

Social

People in the **social** category are known as "helpers." If you are a social person you like to work with people and even may have an interest in healing or developing others. Social people also enjoy teaching, training, and informing others. If you are a social personality type you probably enjoy serving, greeting, and interacting with others. Common personality traits shared by social people include being cooperative, friendly, sociable, and understanding. If this is you, then you would do well in a career focused on communicating orally or via writing, supporting others, training, teaching, coaching, and informing others. There are many communication careers that align with this personality type, including the following: spokesperson, brand ambassador, corporate trainer, teacher, community liaison, professional career/executive coach, public speaking coach, and writer. Several years ago there was a boom in consulting firms focusing on providing public speaking skills training to CEOs and presidents of companies. Boston was one city where this explosion of communication training took place. If you are one of the few who truly enjoys and excels at public speaking, you could use that talent to help others improve their dislike of and weak speaking abilities. Remember much of the nation does not like public speaking; they fear it more than death or spiders!

Enterprising

People in the **enterprising** category are known as "persuaders." If you are persuader you like working with people, influencing others, performing, and leading organizations. You probably like competitive environments. Common traits shared by enterprising people include being ambitious, domineering, energetic, and self-confident. If this is you, you would do well in a career combined with business, such as marketing and sales. You might also quite naturally be attracted to politics and current events. Since enterprising people tend to be extroverted and persuasive, many fields use them in some role to support their mission. For example, a patient advocate looks out for the interests of the patient in a hospital. The patient advocate will work with doctors and insurance companies to present the best interests of the patient. Adjudicators and hearing officers conduct hearings to recommend or make decisions on claims related to government matters. They determine liability, sanctions, or penalties and recommend the acceptance or rejection of claims or settlements. Similar position can be found in insurance companies. Advertisers and promotors are other careers that align with the enterprising personality type. They plan and coordinate advertising policies and programs or produce collateral materials for an organization. If you like to interact with customers, then customer service representative may be a good career option. Customer serve representatives and directors interact with customers to provide information about services and products. Often, they handle complaints and resolve conflict. Many large companies have well-structured customer service departments with layers of leadership, and it is a career that has advancement potential. Think about Walt Disney World, Target, Amazon, and other large companies that must have a clear process for handling and responding customer feedback. There are many different areas of work that match enterprising peoples' interests in working with others. A communication degree will position you well to enter a career upon graduation in an enterprising environment.

Conventional

People in the **conventional** category are known as "organizers." If you are an organizer you probably like structured jobs and working with numbers and instructions. Conventional people generally like to organize data and write reports. If you are a conventional person, you might like to collect things. Common personality traits shared by conventional types include being practical, well-controlled, sociable, conservative, persistent, and conforming. They also tend to be detail oriented and good with numbers. If this is your personality type you thrive in ordered environments with rules and standards that are enforced. There are many careers that align with the interests and abilities of the conventional personality type, including management, information technology, telecommunications, desktop publishing, child development, website editing, and computer programming.

FIGURE 2.2 Holland's Six Personality and Environment Types

EXERCISE 2.4
Working With Your Interests

Answer the following questions. Be as honest and specific as you can.

After reflecting on each question, consider what your answer tells you about your future career. Each question serves as a guide informing you what you might like integrated into your career. Your answers to each of the questions shed light on what you are interested in; some of the interests may connect to your future career. A former student once told me of her love for music. I encouraged him to explore career options connected to his interest in music. Now, he works at a larger radio station doing social media. The answers to the following questions hold invaluable clues to what may be your future career.

(continued ...)

1. How do you spend your down time?

2. What do you daydream about?

3. What activities have you participated in (academic, cultural, social, service, and spiritual) that have impacted you in some positive way?

4. What are your three favorite classes you have taken? Which ones do you most dread?

5. What accomplished are you most proud of?

6. What current event or topic most interests you? Which one concerns you?

7. If you were asked to declare an expertise in something, what would it be?

8. If you could write a book about anything, what would it be about?

9. If you could have someone's job, who would it be, and what would they do?

10. When someone asks you what you want to do when you graduate, how do you answer?

What Is Your Skillset?

The last element, along with values and interests, of knowing yourself that forms the foundation of your career choice is **skill**. As mentioned, collectively, values, interests, and skills provide a path to your career discovery. Through your experiences both inside and outside the classroom over the last 18-plus years you have gained competencies across many areas. What are the accomplishments you have achieved over your lifetime? What talents do you have that enabled you to be successful? These talents are usually transferable skills, which are skills that don't belong to a specific job or industry. Transferable skills are skills that don't belong to a specific job or industry; they are needed across different types of job and industries. As a communication major you already have acquired many transferable skills. Written and oral communication, problem-solving, and teamwork are all examples of transferable skills. Recruiters have identified many transferable skills that are good to have (Indeed, 2021). Following are eight transferable skills and a description of how you can acquire (and demonstrate) them during your college years.

Business Strategy

Business strategy refers to the basic understanding of business processes. As a communication major it is important to see the big picture of how communication operates in an organization. Even if at first thought you don't think you are "going into business," think again. All applications of communication live in a business, whether it be a for-profit or non-profit organization. For example, a radio personality should be knowledgeable about sponsors and how giving away free concert tickets benefits the radio station. A public relations officer needs to understand how all marketing and advertising impacts the budget. As a communication graduate on the job market you will impress your potential employer with your understanding and experience with business processes.

Ideas for gaining knowledge and experience in business strategy include using elective credits to take a business administration, management, human resources, marketing, or accounting class. Consider a minor in business or a related field, such as marketing. Complete an internship. Many programs require internships; if so consider doing one for more than three credits if allowed by your university, or complete two internships. Consider running for treasury for a student club or organization. Participate in organizing a fundraiser for a student club or organization or a nonprofit. Find a business professional who would agree to serve as your mentor. One of the most important pieces of advice is to read. Read everything you can get your hands on discussing current events, the marketplace, businesses, and the economy. It is important to become informed about the world around you and the businesses that live in it. Suggested reads include *Fortune, Harvard Business Review, Forbes, Bloomberg Businessweek, Money, Wired,* and *The Economist.*

Time Management

I once heard that an undergraduate degree demonstrates your ability to use an alarm and manage your schedule. I think that is selling short the value of higher education, but I agree in the importance of having solid time-management skills. Organizations know the value of employees' use of effective time management skills. Plenty of research shows a positive connection between time management and productivity. This is no news to you. I am sure you have kept a list once or more in your life. Whether you created a list of things to pack for college or a grocery list, you probably were more efficient when using a list. I know a clear organized list for the grocery store prepares me for my journey down the aisle. And we have all seen memes about going into Target for one item and leaving with a cart full of items. The truth is college is one of the best times to strengthen your skills. You are already juggling a full class load, usually five classes, and social events. You know exactly how much time it takes you to walk across campus, when to arrive at campus to find a parking space, and the best times for eating at the cafeteria. All of these exhibit time management; however, these are not exactly the examples future employers want to hear. Instead, employers want to see that you are skilled at making a plan and organizing resources (including time) to complete specific tasks. Good time management consists of tactics for executing tasks under pressure.

Ideas for strengthening your time management skills during your college years include sometimes choosing the tougher course, having a double major, working while going to school, participating in a sport, and community service. All of these contribute to the narrative you will give during job interviews. If available, look into completing a directed study type of course in which you will have the opportunity to study and work one-on-one with a faculty member. This opportunity will demonstrate many different things to an employer. You will have a specific example of when you independently sought out an opportunity to seek advance study of a topic of interest. It will also demonstrate time management as well as relationship management with a supervisor. They will also give you experience to draw upon when answering open-ended interview questions. It is commonplace that interviews include situation-based questions. For example, you may hear, "Talk about how you were able to limit distractions to complete your tasks and goals" or "Tell me about a time when you were unable to complete a task on time, and explain why." Both of these situation-based questions require a substantive answer. You will want to demonstrate your ability to manage complex tasks and personal and professional growth. Limiting distractions is something you have practice doing throughout your college years. Sometimes you cannot attend a sporting event or another function because you have to complete a paper. If you are being asked for an example of when you were unable to complete a task on time, consider describing how you became interested in learning the full scope of a situation but you ended up down a rabbit hole. The idea of a "rabbit hole" shows that you have interest in the task and doing your best at it. It also can show that you are willing to learn how to use guard rails to keep you on track. Resist the temptation to blame others for your failures; take ownership of your strengths and weaknesses.

Adapting to Change

Nobody knows better about the need for adapting to change than communication professionals (and students). Communication today is heavily influenced by technology. Technology, as you know, evolves rapidly, and organizations often have a hard time keeping up with the changes. We are living in the age of information fueled by the **knowledge economy**. This refers to the economy relying on the quantity, quality, and accessibility of information available. The knowledge economy will be discussed later when we examine the skill of problem-solving. Being able to adapt to change demonstrates your ability to be resourceful, analytical, and determined. Research in mediation reveals how important adaptability is to one's health and ability to reduce stress. Employers are looking for balanced employees who can manage stress and approach change with a positive attitude (Peart, 2019). Your ability to do this contributes to the overall culture of the organization.

There are many ways to show your adaptability during a job interview. Think about times when you came up with alternative solutions. Imagine how you will be able to talk about how you handled the uncertainty, disruption, and surprises that came along with COVID-19. It is likely your school, regardless of grade, made adjustments and suspended face-to-face classes for nearly half a semester. Consider times when you adapted to new roles. Maybe it was during COVID-19. Many students had to secure new resources, such as computers, internet, and quiet locations just to participate in virtual classes. Not to mention many of us needed to juggle work and caretaking responsibilities. Through your stories of adapting to change you will be able to emphasize your calmness along with your confidence. Employers are looking for employees who can change with the world around us.

Problem-Solving

Easily one of the top skills that recruiters and employers look for in candidates is effective problem-solving (Indeed, 2020, 2021). Truth be told, organizations lose millions of dollars a year as a result of poor problem- solving (Society for Human Resource Management, 2013). The knowledge economy is directly related to problem-solving ability. It emphasizes the use of critical and complex thinking and deemphasizes the skills of repetition, routine, and memorization of industry. Problem-solving is an umbrella skill in that it encompasses several other skills, such as communication, leadership, adaptability, analysis, and the like. It is not uncommon to be asked an open-ended question about your problem-solving skills during an interview. It is important to reflect on the many times you encountered challenges over the course of your personal life, work life, and school life. Two key aspects of problem-solving are creative thinking and overcoming obstacles. Researchers have identified steps for effective problem solving; it is important to remember these steps, so when you are in an interview you will integrate them into the description of successfully solving a problem. The steps include identifying the issues or understanding what the problem is; knowing and understanding others' interests; brainstorming alternative solutions or options; evaluating the options; selecting a solution or option; documenting the agreement or the solution; selecting and agreeing on the process of implementation; and monitoring and evaluating the chosen solution. You will notice the process is logical and detail orientated.

There are many ways you can acquire opportunities to showcase your problem-solving skills. Look for classes that test and strengthen your skills, such as upper-level math classes, economics classes, fundraising classes, campaigning classes, and criminal justice classes. If you are not able to add such classes as electives, look for other ways to demonstrate your ability to tackle problems. Other opportunities may be related to clubs and organizations of which you are a member or from your workplace. Either through a club, organization, or class look for problems or issues on campus or in the surrounding area that you feel need to be addressed. Follow the problem-solving steps previously discussed, and address the problem, either solo or with others. For example, high school students in the area may not be able to afford the clothing for prom. Due to this limitation they often have to skip prom. Organize a formal and semi-formal clothing drive, and open a Cinderella closet. With your campus radio station plan and execute a listen-a-thon or supply the music for a dance-a-thon. Freedom of Speech week is a perfect event to organize and host on campus. At one of the universities where I advised Lambda Pi Eta, the communication honorary, and with students organized a week-long discussion of the city's homeless issue. The students organized a panel discussion with members of the homeless community (also known as "tent city") and nonprofits associated with providing services for the homeless. The debate team organized a debate on the effectiveness and ethics of the city's policy of "bussing" homeless individuals out of the city with a prepaid bus tick and a small amount of money. The student even showed the movie *Homeless to Harvard* and had a guest speaker, a student who was homeless before joining the university as a student. There are many issues worthy of your time and effort to create positive change for others. Look for ways to use class assignments and projects to showcase problem-solving.

Teamwork

In the 1990s "teamwork" became a buzz word for companies. It is just as important now; however, adding "team player" on your resume probably won't help it advance you in the search. Employers want to learn about ways you have experienced being a good follower as well as leader. It is important to keep in mind the group communication research on **small group development** (Miller & Poston, 2020). Groups go through five stages of development, including forming, storming, norming, performing, and adjourning. Did you know that the average task-oriented team stays in the forming stage for about 2 months or more? The forming stage includes examining the skills, strengths, and interests of each member; understanding project goals and timelines; understanding individual roles; and having a discussion and acceptance of group rules. This means all groups you work in, whether in class, club, or work, do not reach the second stage of development for about 2 months. Notice that performing does not happen until the group reaches the fourth stage. Link this information with the fact that the average semester lasts three months; most teams in classes never really reach the point of performing. Your experience might be more appropriately described as "surviving"! All this to say, it is important to be mindful of how you celebrate your experiences in working in teams for a class project. When preparing for entering the internship or job market it is recommended that you think of experiences in teams that have lasted at least 6 months. It would be beneficial to be able to talk about the team's progress through the five stages of development. It is common that interview questions focus on one or more of the stages. The more you become familiar with the stages the more content you will have to include in your responses. For more information on groups and teams read the chapters on small groups in Miller and Poston's 2020 textbook, *Exploring communication in the Real World*.

Teamwork, as a skill, is often talked about like people talk about communication. It is common place to hear people self-proclaim that they are good at communicating with others or that they are "a people person." Yet you know as future communication professionals that there is more to communication than liking to talk or be around people. Often, people reduce the complexity of effective teamwork to its simplest terms. Look at teamwork as a collaborative activity. Teamwork consists of accepting responsibility for your work and collaborating with others, being open to ideas of others, building rapport, and building effective protocols for communicating.

Leadership

Think about the earlier discussion about organizational culture. Leadership plays an important role in organizational culture, although many argue that culture grows from the grassroots and is not imposed by leaders. Looking at it from this perspectives sheds light on why employers are interested in leaders able to work with others to nurture a healthy culture as well as achieve goals with positive outcomes. Also employers look for candidates who have leadership skills or the potential to lead because they tend to be long-term hires, loyal, dedicated, and consistent, which often results in less absences. All of these benefit the organization in many ways, including building an internal source of future leaders and reducing costs.

You might be thinking to yourself that you don't have time in your busy schedule for taking classes and working to become a leader on campus. This may be true, but there are many different things you can do to gain useful skills to support your potential to be a great leader in your future career. An effective and strong leader is discipline. As a college student you naturally have discipline. Remember all those classes you are taking? And what about the roles you have outside of the classroom and off campus? Balancing it all—even if during midterms you may lose your mind—is a skill, and it demonstrates discipline. Are you a member of a sports team? College student-athletes are required to be disciplined. Even if you do not play sports in college, maybe you go running every morning. This shows discipline. Now, these may not be resume items, but they are ingredients of your career path narrative. Don't forget some of the previous items presented in this chapter, such as getting involved in clubs and organizations, can show your potential for leadership. Taking on more projects and managing them is another component of effective leadership. Be a great follower because followership and leadership are different sides of the same coin; they have an interdependent relationship. Great leaders know when to be a great follower. Another way to you can develop your potential for being a great leader is by strengthening your awareness of the situation—the big picture. This awareness is often referred to as "situational awareness." As a communication major you have studied the importance of context. Understanding context helps you identify the variables or factors that influence a situation. This skill demonstrates that you are able to anticipate potential challenges and problems.

If you are a strong student, you should consider finding ways to guide others, such as tutoring. Tutoring on campus will help you build coaching skills, motivational skills, and mentoring skills.

Written and Oral Communication

I am pretty sure you just let out a celebratory sigh and thought, "I picked the right major." Exactly. Communicating effectively might be the most essential employability skill. The majority of jobs require some level of competence in communicating. Everything you learned in your Introduction to Communication class, or similar class about the transactional nature of communication, provides you with the basis of being a competence communicator. The following model (see Figure 2.3) represents the oral communication process; however, you can see how it could be applied to written communication as well. All the factors in the model impact the effectiveness of the communication—oral or written. The ability to successfully participate in this process shows a level of communication competence. To improve competence, effort should be put forth to become aware of patterns of communication and adapt as appropriate to the context or situation.

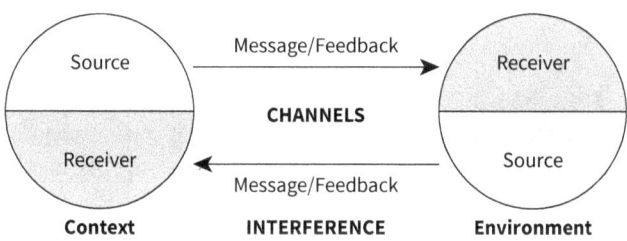

FIGURE 2.3 Transactional Model of Communication

As a communication major you are already building a portfolio of evidence of your oral and written communication competence. I would highly recommend you create a digital portfolio if it is not already a requirement for your degree. There are many companies that offer free portfolio hosting. A few of the most common free sites include Wix, Weebly, and Squarespace. I recommend researching the following options to determine which fits your needs the best. Behance (www.behance.net) is a popular service that has millions of users. This site is best for showcasing visual communication, such as graphic design, photography, Adobe Photoshop, Adobe Illustrator, game design, and audio. An invaluable feature of Behance is the ability to interact with others and get feedback. This will allow you improve your portfolio, so it is at its best come graduation. A similar website to check out is Dribbble (www.dribbble.com). Dribbble allows you to build portfolios for animation, mobile, product design, typography, web design, and branding. This site has the added benefit of accessing designer communities via Dribbble Meetups. You might consider using both accounts. You can build a Dribbble portfolio and add a link to your Behance portfolio. This allows you to benefit from the network of both sites, increasing your odds of being seen and ultimately hired! There are other free portfolio services, such as Adobe Portfolio and Coroflot. If you are not the creative type, and you are looking for a website to host your public relations portfolio, you may want to check out Crevado (www.crevado.com). Crevado allows you to upload various file types, including photo, video, audio, animated GIF, PDF, and Adobe Shockwave. This site offers Google Analytics reporting, which is excellent for tracking views of your portfolio. This site would allow you to upload speeches, press releases, media kits, and many other items. Crevado offers a limited free trial, and then it charges a fee. Remember information is power. You can always design a blog, website, social media, and so on, but you will be responsible for gaining traction for your site. Portfolios, along with building your personal brand, will be discussed in the next chapter.

Data Analysis

It is important to make data-driven decisions. Organizations rely on information and data when making decisions. As an employee you will be expected to have skills in making sound decisions based on data. Proficient data analysis skills include the ability to interpret information, extracting results, and creating reports. One example of this in the communication field is an earned media report. Communication directors of organizations, for-profit as well as non-profit, create earned media reports to summarize media coverage that the organization received over a period of time, often quarterly or annually. This report provides an overview of the different types of media coverage the organization and its employees received. It often includes press coverage, social media mentions, shares and retweets, product or service reviews, blog posts, interviews, and influencer shout-outs. The activity captured in the report are those that are organic or authored or created outside the organization. There are many different types of metrics that communication professionals use to show value. Professionals want to show the value of **communication collateral** purchased by an organization. Understanding social media from an organizational perspective, not as a consumer, is helpful.

What should you being doing during college to gain data analytics skills? I would suggest taking a social media marketing, web analytics, or data mining class. If you don't have room in your graduation plan to take extra courses, try learning data analytics online. One resource to check out is edX data analysis and statistics courses. The courses are self-paced and free (if you do not want a certificate). Via edX (www.edx.org/search), MITx offers a course titled The Analytics Edge, which teaches the power of data. Interning at an organization that has the opportunity to teach you and mentor you in data analytics would be a great way to gain some experience.

When reflecting on the listed transferable skills it is important to recognize how they weave together in your story. Remember the job interview is an application of narrative theory. You are the architect and teller of your story. The more convincing your story is the more likely you will advance as a top candidate and ultimately be hired. It is natural to think about competency when talking about skills. Since the first time you entered a classroom, educators have been determining your competency. In kindergarten, they wanted to know if you could complete life skills, such as tie your shoe. As you grew, the skills that were measured changed. You were assessed on your competency to do algebra. Figure 2.4 shows the levels of competency based on Curtiss and Warren's early work (1973).

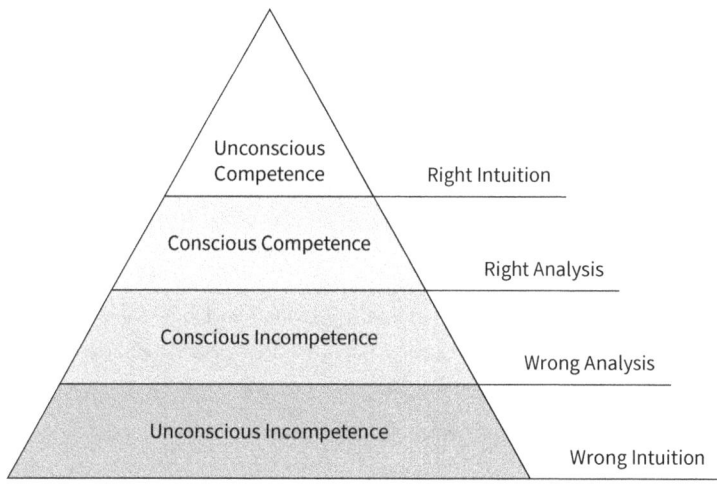

FIGURE 2.4 The Hierarchy of Competence

The hierarchy of competence model shows that as you learn a particular skill you move up the four levels of competence. Unknowingly making small mistakes is an example of **unconscious incompetence**, whereas **conscious incompetence** is making mistakes repeatedly and being aware that you are making the mistakes. You are aware of the mistakes, which allows you the opportunity to address them later. Unconscious incompetence is often thought of by others as you not knowing what you don't know. Once you gain proficiency you advance to the level of conscious competence. In this level you still make small amount of mistakes, whereas the level of unconscious competence is considered mastery. Performing skills at this level requires less effort on your part. As a college student it should be your goal to assess your skills, determine your deficiencies, and make a plan for moving up the levels of competency. This should be a lifelong effort to increase competency across new skills.

EXERCISE 2.5
Conducting a Skills Gap Analysis

In this exercise you will be trying to align your skills with the needs and demands of the job market. You will complete several steps:

1. Think of a job you think you might like to have upon graduating. Let's say you are interested in being a community liaison. You like that this job uses your communication degree and is primarily responsible for managing communication between the public and an organization, such as a police department, school, or nonprofit.
2. Once you have a job in mind look for at least five advertisements for open positions for a community liaison. The jobs can be located anywhere, or you can focus on the place you would most like to live after graduation. It is recommended that you find at least one local opening.
3. Complete the following table, extracting information from the job position.
4. Grab a current copy of your resume. If you don't have one use this as an opportunity to visit your university's career center. They will help you develop a resume.
5. Using the completed table determine how much your resume is aligned with the requirements of the jobs you selected.
6. Make a plan to gain or strengthen skill competency.

Complete the following plan. Be creative in thinking of ways you can do something that would demonstrate the required skills. These ways could include taking a class, declaring a minor, volunteering, taking an online class, using class projects or assignments, internships, summer jobs, and the like. I highly recommend that you speak with your academic advisor or a faculty member. Share what you discovered, and ask for feedback. The faculty will have suggestions and might introduce you to a mentor. Revisit the results of this **skills gap** activity each semester and in the summer. Keep track of skills gained, and be sure to add them to your resume. Updating your resume is something you should do often.

(continued ...)

CHAPTER 2 Identifying Your Values, Interests, and Skills

Job Overview			
	Job #1	Job #2	Job #3
Position			
Company & Location			
Required Qualifications			
Preferred Qualifications			
Responsibilities			
Nature of the Work			
Other Information (Salary, Travel, etc.)			
Transferable Skills			

Skills Acquisition Plan	
Fall	Spring

(continued ...)

Fall	Spring
Fall	Spring
Fall	Spring

Summer and Winter Breaks

SPOTLIGHT ON COMMUNICATION
Identity

This chapter has emphasized how it is important to understand different aspects of yourself. The **self** is a concept communication researchers have long examined. The communication theory of identity (Hecht et al., 2005) asserts that identity is perpetuated by and through communication. Communication plays an essential role in how our identity is co-constructed with and through our social environment. In other words, our identity is influenced by society. We learn who we are through interaction with others, including the media. Communication is a dynamic process, and so is our identity. Consider how you might describe your identity as a 5 year old or a 16 year old. Would you describe your identity as being the same then as it is now? Probably not.

(continued ...)

There is a dynamic aspect to our identity as we age and gain more experiences. We also have multiple identities. Who we are at work differs from who we are among our family. This is connected to the different identities we have. Identity also is created in spurts. Often the milestones in our lives are aligned with one of these spurts. You might recall when you started driving and had more freedom or when you got your first job. You probably started to view yourself differently because you were evolving from childhood into adulthood. It makes sense to think that our values, interests, and skills are connected to our identity. If you have a special talent or skill, it becomes part of your identity. You often hear people say, "I am a cat person" or "I am a dog person." This interest in a specific type of pet becomes part of how we identify ourselves. I am a dog person! As you examine your values, interests, and skills remember most likely they will change over time—including during your college years.

Self-concept is closely related to identity. Rogers (1959) argued that one's self-concept actually has three parts: You have a view of yourself, which is your **self-image**. You also place value on yourself, which is your **self-esteem** or **self-worth**. Lastly, you also have an image of what you wish you were like; this is your **ideal self**. Together, all three form how you see and evaluate yourself.

Rogers also identified five characteristics of a functioning person. Being open to experiences, both positive and negative, is the first characteristic. Throughout this book it is emphasized that owning and investing in your college experience will not only foster personal development but also professional growth. The second characteristic is existential living, which refers to being connected to different experiences in your life and not advoiding or judging experiences. The heart of this is living in the moment and not ruminating on the past. As a college student it is likely that you will encounter something negative, such as a poor grade. Reflect, learn, and move forward. The third characteristic is trusting your feelings. As humans we have feelings; learn to trust your instincts. It is not uncommon for some communication majors to have started out as another major. If you were in another major, you probably trusted your feeling that it was not a fit, and you switched majors. As you begin to interview for internships and jobs, remember to trust your instincts. Not all jobs or organizations are good fits. Creativity is the fourth characteristic of functioning people. Creative thinking includes a certain amount of risk-taking. Allow yourself to be creative in how you think about your college career and post-college career. Embrace the ability to adjust, adapt, and change. Continue to look for new challenges and experiences, in the classroom, outside the classroom, and in your career. Finally, having a fulfilled life is vital to being a functioning person. This is being happy and satisfied with like. This is ultimately the goal of this book. You should experience college and strategically prepare yourself for life after college all for the purpose of loving your future career and the life it helps you build.

TOOLS FOR GAINING INSIGHT IN YOURSELF

Here is a list of resources to watch and read. Each reinforces the topics presented in the chapter.

Phil Hansen (2013): "Embrace the Shake"

Phil Hansen, an artist, has a 2013 TED Talk that inspires us to see our interest in a new way. He shares the story of how, as an artist, he suffered from an injured hand. This forces him to find another way to engage in art, something he loved. He shares many photos of the art he created by using nontraditional methods. I found his story to be quite inspirational.

WATCH AT https://www.ted.com/talks/phil_hansen_embrace_the_shake

Holland Code (RIASEC) Test

This is a free test that will allow you to see what category of careers you may be best suited for. Take the test, and reflect on your results. Explore your results and how they may inform the path to your future career.

READ AT https://openpsychometrics.org/tests/RIASEC/

National Career Development Association

This webpage has links to many different resources for career development. There are links to self-assessments, general career information, and much more.

READ AT https://www.ncda.org/aws/NCDA/pt/sp/resources

(continued ...)

Career Resources for College Students With Disabilities

This website has useful information for college students with disabilities. There is information about recruitment programs and leadership programs geared toward students with disabilities. These invaluable resources can serve as a connector to resources for being matched with an internship and job.

READ AT https://www.nccsdclearinghouse.org/career-page-for-students.html

Bill Lindstaedt (2018): "The Fantasy, the Ideal, and the Reality of Career Exploration"

Bill Lindstaedt, of UCSF's Office of Career and Professional Development, shares information and experiences about exploring careers. It is a short, engaging video.

WATCH AT https://www.youtube.com/watch?v=d-DoNgtfNcc

KEY TERMS

artistic: From John Holland's RIASEC theory, artistic refers to people who are creative and innovative. Common personality traits shared by artistic people include being imaginative, disorderly, idealistic, emotional, and sometimes impractical.

broad values: Broad values are often called personal values and these values usually transfer across specific contexts.

business strategy: Business strategy refers to the basic understanding of business processes.

communication collateral: Anything message you create to enhance the brand of a company or person. Also referred to as marketing collateral. There are many different pieces of collateral. Some examples include, social media post and videos, email, newsletters, presentations, magazines, white papers, and the like.

conscious incompetence: Conscious incompetence is making mistakes repeatedly and being aware that you are making the mistakes.

conventional: From John Holland's RIASEC theory conventional career people are known as "organizers."

core values: Principles that guide a person's behavior and their relationship with the world around them. This principle is considered to be fundamental to what the person sees as being important.

enterprising: From John Holland's RIASEC theory, enterprising people are known as "persuaders."

extrinsic values: Extrinsic values refer to tangible rewards you receive from your career. The most common example of extrinsic rewards you receive from work is money/pay.

ideal self: The image of what you wish you were like is your ideal self.

interests: Interests refers to the things you have a desire to learn more about or spend more time doing.

intrinsic values: Intrinsic values refer to what motivates you internally to do the what you do such as work. When applying core values to your future career, intrinsic values motivate you do the work you do.

investigative: From John Holland's RIASEC theory, investigative people are thinkers. They like to observe, learn, analyze, evaluate, and problem-solve.

knowledge economy: An economy relies on the quantity, quality, and accessibility of information available.

lifestyle values: Lifestyle values refer to how you want to live. These values determine your lifestyle.

realistic: From John Holland's RIASEC theory, realistic people are doers. Realistic people are likely prefer physical activities requiring skills, strength, and often coordination.

RIASEC theory: John Holland, a psychologist, developed a theory that suggests that people can be described as six personality types. The personality types include realistic, investigative, artistic, social, enterprising, and conventional.

self: The self is the way in which you view yourself that is co-constructed with and through our social enviornment.

self-esteem or self-worth: Self-esteem or self-worth is the value you place on yourself. This is one of three parts that make up your self-concept.

self-image: Self-image is your view of oneself and is one of three parts that make up your self-concept.

skills: Skills are the things you are able to do well. Having skill at something usually means you have some level of expertise.

skills gap: Skill gap refers to the missing skills required by a certain job or industry. To determine your skills gap compare the list of skills on your resume with the "must have" skills listed in advertised open positions for a job. If the job is asking for something you do not have on your resume, there is a gap.

small group development: Small group development most commonly refers to the 5 stages that a group goes through as the people work together. The five stages are known as forming, storming, norming, performing, and adjourning.

social: From John Holland's RIASEC theory, social people are helpers. Social people like to work with people and even may have an interest in healing or developing others.

think tank: A think tank refers to a body of experts that provide research, advice and recommendations on specific social issues, political and economic problems. The most influential think tanks in the USA include: Belfer Center for Science and International Affairs, Earth Institute, Heritage Foundation, Human Rights Watch, Kaiser Family Foundation, Council on Foreign Relations, American Enterprise Institute, RAND Corporation and Center for Strategic and International Studies.

unconscious incompetence: When you unknowingly making small mistakes.

values: Values is a general term referring to a person's belief how one should behavior. Also reflects what the person views as being important in life and/or work.

CREDITS

Fig. 2.1b: Copyright © by Three Six Five, (CC BY 3.0) at https://thenounproject.com/term/ruler/1725424/.

Fig. 2.2b: Copyright © by Bonegolem, (CC BY 3.0) at https://thenounproject.com/search/?q=hammer&i=532224.

Fig. 2.2c: Copyright © by Chris Homan, (CC by 3.0) at https://thenounproject.com/term/gear-head/600339/.

Fig. 2.2d: Copyright © by Maxim Kulikov, (CC by 3.0) at https://thenounproject.com/term/lightbulb/1263005/.

Fig. 2.2e: Copyright © by Muhammad Ridho, (CC by 3.0) at https://thenounproject.com/term/hand-holding-heart/3772279/.

Fig. 2.2f: Copyright © by Adrien Coquet, (CC by 3.0) at https://thenounproject.com/term/advice/2217256/.

Fig. 2.2g: Copyright © by froz, (CC by 3.0) at https://thenounproject.com/term/iphone/28974/.

Fig. 2.4: Copyright © by TylzaeL (CC BY-SA 4.0) at https://commons.wikimedia.org/wiki/File:Competence_Hierarchy_adapted_from_Noel_Burch_by_Igor_Kokcharov.svg.

CHAPTER 3

Building Your Personal Brand

It has always been understood that there are benefits to managing your reputation. Think back your time as a student. When you were younger, you were less aware of the idea of a reputation, although you were very much aware when other children did not like you or did not play with you. You might have been aware of the concept of privacy. As you grew and advanced through middle and high school, you likely became more aware of reputation. It is during these years that you probably made your first real attempts to manage your reputation. These ideas translate to your reputation in college and beyond. In this chapter, 21st-century tools will be discussed for building your reputation and entering the job market. Four specific tools will be discussed, including personal branding, social media, a video resume or cover letter, and a portfolio.

Creating a Personal Brand

Over the decades we have gained an understanding of reputation and how it changes not only over time but among different stakeholders. In more current times reputation management has taken a focus on building a **personal brand**, which means you should think of yourself as a product. Consider your some of your favorite products. What qualities do they possess that influences why you like them? We all have different attitudes and beliefs about the products based on our unique experiences. Products that are strong are usually thought of as being authentic, visible, and valuable. Also, we usually gravitate toward products that are consistent. I cannot help but think of the paper towel commercial that compares the generic towel with the "national" brand. The name brand always outperforms the generic brand. Think about that wording: name brand. This terminology is used because the product is made by a source that we recognize by name. Be the name brand. This is not to say that unknown brands of products are always lesser, but it does suggest that sometimes it may take longer for unknown brands to be selected. This translates to job hunting. Sometimes the "underdog" will get the job offer over the candidate with the better resume. Jeff Bezos, an American industrialist and the founder, CEO, and president of the online retail company Amazon stated, "Your brand is what people say about you when you're not in the room" (Arruda, 2016). I think it is sound advice to build your personal brand, so people think of you when they hear about a job opportunity. You will be relying on the opinions of others to get your first post-graduation job. You will want faculty and staff to share news of open positions. You will also want them to write letters and serve as references. These are all easier when you are known. The qualities of your favorite products also apply to your own personal brand.

> **EXERCISE 3.1**
> **You As a Product**
>
> In the box write a description of yourself as if you were a product. What are the features and qualities that make you the preferred product over competitors?

Why is personal brand so important? It is key because you will have more control over your destiny. With a strong brand you will be able to differentiate yourself from others, which is necessary when competing for a job in the marketplace. You will be able to maximize your career potential. When others hold you in high regard it is likely to influence their desire to work with you, either now or in the future.

Building and managing your personal brand requires responsibility. To get ahead you will need to manage the impressions others have of you. This starts in college.

> **SPOTLIGHT ON COMMUNICATION**
> **Elaboration Likelihood Model**
>
> Petty and Cacioppo (1980) proposed the elaboration likelihood model, or the ELM, as a theory of persuasion. "Elaboration" refers to the amount of effort a person needs to use to attach meaning to a message and ultimately accept it or reject it. Briefly stated, the ELM describes persuasion as consisting of two distinct processes: the central route and the peripheral route. Individuals process different messages in different ways. Depending on how they process the message determines whether persuasion was reached and attitude changed. The central route requires more effort and includes analyzing the content of the message. Central-route thinking is similar to examining and evaluating a message's *logos*, whereas the peripheral route requires less effort of elaboration. The person does not analyze or scrutinize the message for effectiveness or detail; instead, the person looks for other cues to assign meaning.
>
> The ELM theory is something to consider when building your personal brand and professional pieces, such as portfolio. Your personal brand's intent is persuading others to attend to your message, or hear your message. Students often ask, "How do I get others to read my social media or portfolio?" The answer lies within the ELM theory. You will need to design your messages to include both central and peripheral cues. If someone needs central cues to be persuaded to hire you, be sure your personal brand items include them. Don't forget to include the peripheral cues as well because some will be persuaded not by your message but the way it looks and is presented. For example, one person might just need to see that you graduated from Harvard University (i.e., name recognition, which is a peripheral cue) before offering you the interview, whereas another person may need to see your list of work experience, performance in classes, and the argument you made in your cover letter before offering an interview. As you read through this chapter, keep in mind the ELM theory and different ways you could use it to build a strong persuasive message directed at the industry you hope to work in.

It cannot be expressed enough how important the relationship you have with your faculty is. I encourage you from the very start to make a practice of using office hours. At the start of the semester introduce yourself after the first day of class. Prior to attending the first office hour session do some research on your faculty. In your research examine your university's and program's website, LinkedIn, and Google. Learn about their background, including education, prior teaching experience, research interests, classes they teach, and so on. Being aware of this information allows you to make a personal connection. When you are in their office be sure to observe the items in the office. Maybe you notice photos of international travel or a mascot of a professional team. If you notice that you have something in common, such as a childhood hometown or an interest in a professional sports team, don't be shy about mentioning it. Throughout, make it a priority to participate during class. First this is an effective way to learn, and second it helps continue the professional relationship-building process. I mention "professional relationship" because I think it is helpful to remember that faculty members have a profession (more than a job), and they are in that profession to share their passion: the subject area in which they are experts. Remember most faculty spent years studying in great depth their field, and they often get excited about sharing their joy with students. I know it might be hard to imagine that in your math class, but it is true. Make use of this, and show interest in your classes, even if they are not in your major. You might be surprised at the unexpected rewards.

I mentioned attending office hour sessions. It is good practice to attend at least three sessions throughout a 16-week semester. Be intentional during your visit. Do some planning about what you want to accomplish during your meeting. Do you need help understanding something from class or the homework? Do you want to continue a discussion from class? Do you want advising help on which classes to take or minor to declare? Do you want to share your professional goals? Remember to be respectful of faculty members' time and other students who may be waiting to speak with the faculty during office hours. It goes without saying that attending office hours is important work for a good grade in the class. At the end of the semester, consider making notes about the semester if you intend to ask the faculty member for a letter of recommendation prior to graduation. Be sure to check out your university's website for a page outline tips for building a professional relationship with your faculty. Often, these pages are in student affairs or even the accessibility office. Don't avoid these pages because they provide good information for all students. A YouTube Channel, College Info Greek (2017), released a show, "How to Build a Good Relationship with Your Professor," that provides almost 50 minutes of conversation on the topic. Much useful information is shared.

Table 3.1 provides a template for keeping notes on the relational experiences for each class you take. This is a type of **relational network mapping**. Relational network mapping is a record of people you have worked with and experiences, milestones, and turning points worth remembering. Why do this? By the time you are ready to ask for recommendations and references, you will be prepared to attach context and a story with the way you are coming to the person specifically. You will want to be intentional when you ask for references. Be sure the person can positively and substantively add to your story—your personal brand. Use the following table as a template for keeping notes on faculty you worked well with in and out of class. Include the courses you took with the person or other ways you know the faculty. It is always a good idea to track grades you earned in the classes. Make notes of why the faculty stood out to you. Why did you connect with this person? Lastly, jot down some of the things you did during the semester. Did you attend office hours or study sessions? Did you work on a project that received positive feedback from the faculty? Did you receive other feedback from the faculty in class or on assignments that suggest the person thinks highly of you? Do this exercise every semester. Add others as appropriate, such as house staff, coaches, librarians, and the like. You can even include people you have met throughout your college years off campus. Maybe you volunteered and worked well with the volunteer coordinator. You will find that tracking your relationship will enrich your future interviews. You will have a diary of sorts to refer to before interviewing, and you will have captured moments and situations worth talking about with prospective employers.

TABLE 3.1 **Relational Network Mapping**

Faculty Name	Course Taken	Grade	Impressions	Notes

There are several steps you can take to build your own personal brand. While in college it is a good exercise to complete an audit of your social media. An audit is like an inventory. It is helpful during an audit to look for your name and photos on the internet using a search engine.

To build your personal brand, start by analyzing yourself. What are your strengths? Sometimes it is difficult to recognize our strengths. It is a good idea to speak with friends, family, teachers, coaches, and employers to get a sense of what they view as your strengths. Often, we neglect to see what others see in us. Be sure to keep a list of your strengths. As you add to this list throughout your college years, date your new entry, and add some notes. You will find these notes will be helpful in writing cover letters and preparing for job interviews. One common interview question is about your strengths. You will not only be prepared with an answer but will be able to provide context to your answer. Future employers will value your ability to give a genuine answer and provide context regarding how you came to know your strengths. As you continue to analyze yourself think about what benefits you would bring to a company. It is helpful if you consider this for a few different companies or industries. Many students have a broad job hunt when just starting out. When considering how you will benefit a company, rule number one is using the company's mission statement. In your cover letters and interviews be sure to demonstrate how you can contribute to delivering the company's **mission statement**. A mission defines the company's goals. It can be considered the official statement explaining what a company does, and why the company does it. When hiring, the employer wants to ensure that the prospective employee can contribute to the work of the company.

EXERCISE 3.2
Finding Value in Companies' Mission Statements

Using your favorite search engine look for the top mission statements in the industry you are most interested in. Look for the differences between the statements. Answer the following questions for three mission statements you found:

1. What is the name of the company?

2. What is the mission statement? If long, consider writing the URL for the website where it is written.

3. Pull out the main themes of the mission statement. For example, Disney's statement is the following: "*To entertain, inform and inspire* people *around the globe* through the power of unparalleled *storytelling*, reflecting the *iconic brands, creative minds* and *innovative technologies* that make ours the world's *premier entertainment company*" (Disney, n.d.). I've set the themes in italics.

4. Brainstorm how you could contribute to helping the company deliver its mission statement. What skills, experiences, behaviors, and talents do you have that are aligned with some of the themes. Keep in mind that some mission statements are complex, so not many employees can deliver each and every theme. The more you can demonstrate that your background aligns with mission statement the more competitive a candidate you will be.

5. Reflect on the results. Assess which mission statements you most align with and which you do not. Are you still interested in working for the companies? Why, or why not? If you have misalignments, what can you do to strengthen your alignment with the company's mission? Are these things you can do before you graduate? How will you accomplish this? Compare the results with Exercise 2.5: Conducting a Skills Gap Analysis.

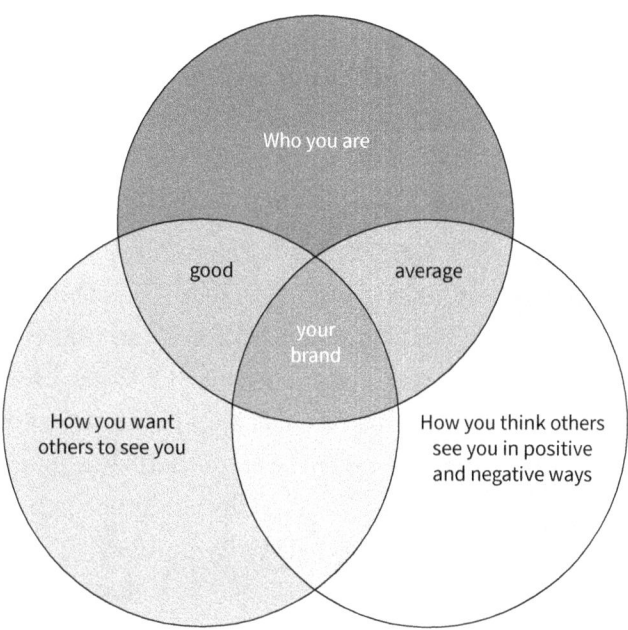

FIGURE 3.1 Your Personal Brand

Figure 3.1 is a visual representation of you as a personal brand. In Exercise 3.3 you will start the process of building your personal brand. College is the perfect time to start building your brand. If you wait until graduation, or after graduation, it will be difficult for two reasons: (1) You will have less support at your fingertips once you leave school, and (2) you will be under the stress of job hunting to spend the time reflecting as you build your brand. To start, think about what your goal is for your education, career, and life. Be sure the personal brand you are building matches with these goals. The ultimate goal of this process is to write your personal brand statement. Start the process of building your personal brand by thinking about your identity. Who are you now? Who do you strive to be in your first career? Think about your attributes. Some attributes that are connected to your personal brand include accessibility or being reachable, attitude, ethics, integrity, professional appearance, open-mindedness, and presentation. When I think about my attributes I think about how I am goofy and have a contagious laugh. I am also ambitious. I have always had big goals for myself. When thinking about your vision, you have already done the heavy lifting in the previous chapter. This about who you are. You will want to set and prioritize your values and identify your passions. Next, consider what value you bring to the workplace. Think about the earlier mission statement exercise; you should see connections on which to build. You are now ready to put your thoughts together and form your personal brand statement. This statement is not a job title; it is aspirational for your life and how you approach it. It is not an advertising slogan aimed at potential consumers. Even though the personal brand may help you in your job hunt it is intended to be authentic and not merely a marketing ploy. To do this, you will write about two sentences with special emphasis on your value (what you are the best at), who you wish to serve (your audience) and future unique promise of value. You want it to be memorable, striking, and solution oriented. Once you are finished, it is helpful to get feedback from others who know you well. Ask yourself, "Is the perception of others consistent with your perception of yourself?" If you have experience in a part-time or summer job, ask trusted colleagues to read over your statement. Look over previous performance reviews before finalizing your statement. In the words of Steve Jobs, "Be a yardstick of quality. Some people aren't used to an environment where excellence is expected" (Vora, 2010).

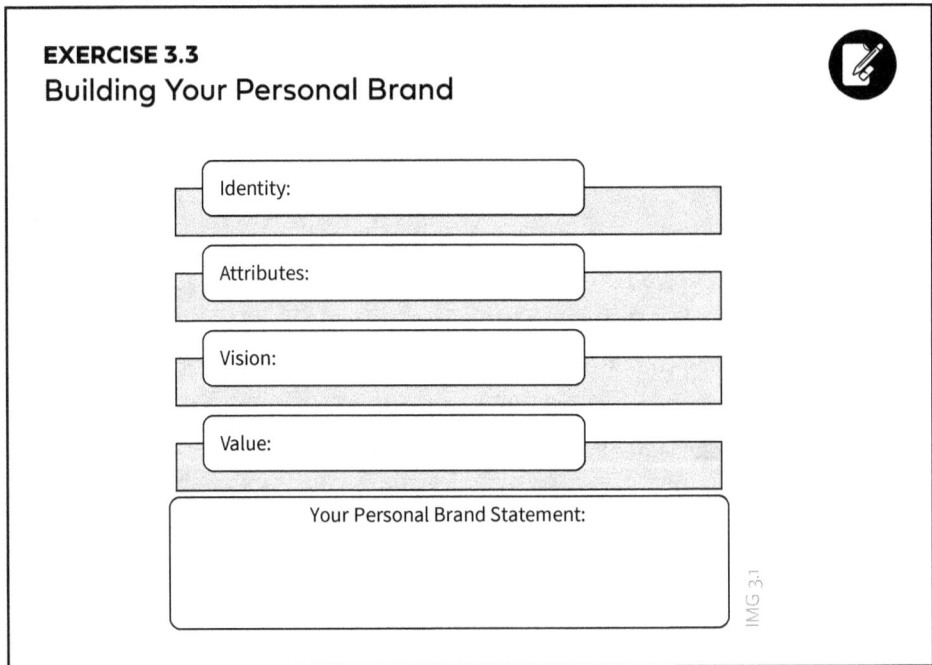

IMG 3.1

Creating a Presence on Social Media

You and your peers probably know how to use social media in your personal lives as consumers. Social media has a lot of power to make (or break) your job search. It is well known that nearly all companies use social media for hiring. Easily three out of four recruiters will check out a candidate's social profiles (Burch, 2021). I have even heard of cases in which the prospective candidate was instructed to accept a friend request from a background investigator. Social media has impacted our personal brand and has given us tools to build it, manage it, and repair it.

If you want to benefit from social media network for your future job search, here are six things to do. First, let people know that you are looking for a job. It is acceptable to add notes on your LinkedIn account stating your career goals and that you are looking for a career position. Keep in mind that, in general, I caution you against using Facebook for work, unless you are using a profile strictly for work. As the old adage goes, avoid mixing business with pleasure. As social media evolves, there often is a generational difference in who uses which platform. Many younger people are not on Facebook; keep in mind your prospective hiring manager might be on Facebook. If you want to use Facebook to scope your business opportunities look at who is in your friends list. Examine your Facebook friends, and classify the friends by creating lists. You can create a list for "work." This will help you target your responses and even your posts. This way only your true friends will see the new pictures of your puppy or the birthday party you attended. Consider how you might use Snapchat in your job search and building your personal brand. According to Tretina (2016), many companies, such as HubSpot Goldman Sachs, Taco Bell, and General Electric, use the platform, which makes it possible to connect with them as a prospective employer. Tretina suggests that you use Snapchat to highlight achievements, tell your story as an emerging professional, network with employers, and gain career development advice. Twitter, like Snapchat, is not just for fun. Use Twitter with more purpose. Join industry-related conversations. Follow the hashtags. This will allow you to follow the trail of open positions. There are several popular job opening hashtags recruiters use to locate prospective applicants. Some of the common ones include #JobSearch, #JobHunt, #NowHiring, #Hiring, #Resume, #JobOpening, and #TweetMyJobs. Table 3.2 lists several Twitter feeds you should consider following. Review the list, and decide which to follow. I suggested you revisit the list every so often to see which new ones to add. When preparing to enter the job market it is best to continually monitor what you are doing and what you can be doing. As you know social media changes rapidly.

TABLE 3.2   **Twitter Feeds to Follow**

Name	Handle	Keywords
Rachel Miller	@AllthingsIC	PR, podcast, job postings
Ben Watts	@wattsnextBen	HR, networking
The Institute of Internal Communication	@IoICNews	Professional promoting internal communication

(continued ...)

Name	Handle	Keywords
Poppulo	@PoppuloSays	Intuitive internal communications, web-based tool
Abby Kohut	@Absolutely_Abby	HR, job-hunting advice
Alison Doyle	@AlisonDoyle	Author, job-hunting source
Journalist'sToolbox	@journtoolbox	Shares digital/data tools, free newsletter
Adam Tinworth	@adders	Digital journalism strategy, training
Columbia Journalism Review	@CJR	Monitoring the press, tracking the evolving media business
CareerBuilder	@CareerBuilder	Career advice, job hunting
Christine Barney	@cmbarney	CEO of rbb Communications
Poynter Institute	@Poynter	Media research, nonprofit, journalism school, fact-checking
Andy Carvin	@acarvin	NPR author, journalist
Dan Gillmor	@dangillmor	Technology writer, columnist
David Banks	@DBanksy	Media law

It is important to create a social media plan. There are several steps to follow to be successful. First, commit to consistent activity. There is nothing worse than social media accounts that are not kept up. This can actually hurt your success. Don't feel you have to have 25 accounts across platforms. It will be important to be strategic. Experts have developed a systematic process for using social media effectively. Second, manage your time. Be realistic about what you can handle and accomplish as you are completing your education. For example, spend 15 minutes a day on your social media activity. For most this is manageable, even during the busy times of the semester. Make it fun and not work. Social media activity can be a stress reliever and a needed break from studying. Following are some benchmarks regarding daily activity you should strive for: Make 1 Facebook post per day Twitter; make 15 tweets per day; make 11 Pinterest pins per day; make 1 LinkedIn post per day; and make 1–2 Instagram posts per day. Keep in mind you will need to work up to this if you are new at social media. You can use these guidelines to set goals for your social media.

Third, use automated scheduling tools. This allows you to have content you can schedule to post automatically. It is a great way to manage your time and still keep your social media active. There are many different tools for scheduling content. Two popular ones include Hootsuite and TweetDeck. Fourth, track your activity; after all, the reason you are doing this is to get people to engage with you on your social media platforms. There are companies that do the tracking for you. Again, there are many out there from which to choose. Keyhole is a useful for monitoring Twitter and Instagram. Hootsuite is popular for monitoring many platforms, including LinkedIn, Twitter, Facebook, Google+, Foursquare, and WordPress. Digimind is interesting because it will monitor and measure sentiment—that is, if people are saying negative, positive, or neutral things about you. Sprout Social is popular for analytics in helping increase activity.

You might be wondering how to develop content for your social media. Your social media does not have to be school related. It does not even have to be career or industry specific. Remember the purpose of using social media is showcasing your varied abilities. You can use the space to display your social media savviness, writing skills, knowledge, and expertise. You are also showcasing your ability to engage with others and create an audience-targeted message. Everything you are learning in the classroom can be on display in "real life." There is no better way to answer an interviewer's question about your persuasive writing skills than by showing a Twitter account with over 100,000 followers. I have said for years that social media influence is persuasion 2.0. Don't discount what a successful social media account demonstrates to potential employers. Plus, it is fun! It should be fun to take aspects of what you are learning and experiencing in college and use it outside of the classroom. You get to practice the concepts and apply the tools in a way that makes sense to you and interests you.

I tell students to start with what interests them. If you love music and going to concerts, then it would make sense to start a music criticism or entertainment site. A music site will showcase your critical thinking skills and ability to assess information. Not to mention, it will provide great writing samples for the potential employer. You should use social media to promote your accomplishments. This will promote potential employers with a glimpse into your abilities and how they are viewed by others. If you have a social media account, you should be active on other social media accounts. Keep in mind people read comments. Maximize your participation by always thinking through your post before posting it (or responding). You might be surprised how many people know their regular contributors. Regularly contributing to social media in a positive, professional manner may be likened to networking at a professional event face to face. It may lead to future opportunities. Be sure to always communicate effectively. I believe communication majors bear that extra burden of being expected to be competent and effective. It is sometimes hard to live down a social media error if not caught quickly. Be sure to proofread. Use templates that work for your social media platform to reduce the chance for errors. Lastly, stay relevant; your content should align with current events and trends.

EXERCISE 3.4
Creating Social Media Content

Step 1: Brainstorming Possible Topics

1. List four topics you are most interested in.
   _____

2. List four topics you would consider yourself experienced or an expert in.
   _____

3. List four things you like to do when you are not in class.
   _____

4. List four things you learned in college that have stuck with you.
   _____

5. List four memorable experiences from your life.
   _____

6. List four people you most admire.
   _____

Step 2: Narrowing the Potential Topics

For each of these prompts, circle the one answer that most interests or sticks out to you. Use these narrowed six topics to practice dreaming about your potential social media theme and content. In each circle think how it could be a theme for your social media.

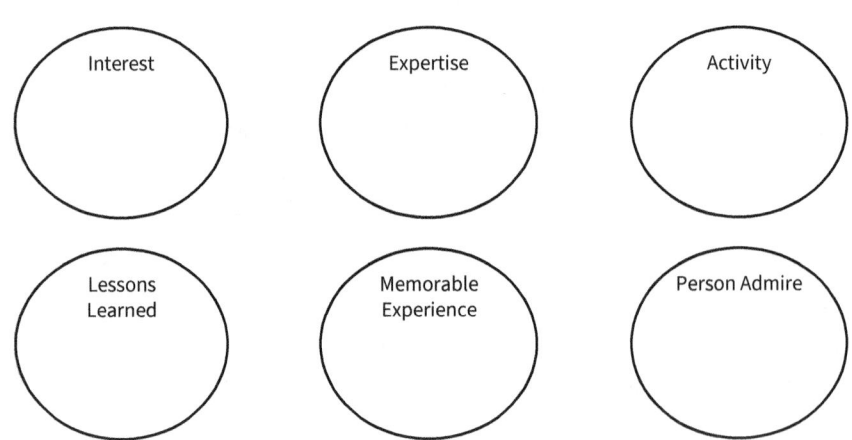

IMG 3.2

Social media is a powerful tool. Most students think of social media as a consumer, rather than a personal branding, tool, or even a business tool. Imagine how you could purposefully use it to gain as stronger entrance into your desired career industry. The core message of this book is to become more strategic during your college years. At the end of the day it is not the piece of paper at graduation that will land you a job. Do not be fooled into thinking that going to class earns you the job. Going to class earns you the diploma. Over my 25 years of teaching in higher education, I have worked with all types of students. The students who are must successful in the job market are those who see opportunity in most things around them. You probably know more about social media platforms than I do—as a consumer. I encourage you to look at what platforms you are already using through a different lens. How are companies using the platforms? Make a list of companies you are interested in working with. Now, go to their website, and see which social media platforms they have a presence on, then go and follow and connect with them. As you continue developing and implementing your vision for your social media there are several articles worth reading (see the New Tools for a New Generation box at the end of the chapter for several articles). Don't forget to add your social profiles to your resume, blog, website, and the like.

Creating a Video Cover Letter

In addition to creating a personal brand and creating a professional presence on social media, there are two things you should create while in college. The first is a **video cover letter**. This is a brief video, about two minutes long, that highlights your resume through a visual and audio message. More and more companies expect communication majors to have the savviness to create a media-rich video. Some companies encourage applicants to submit a video resume with their application. You can find many examples of video cover letters on YouTube. The video cover letter is 1–2 minutes long; it is where you introduce yourself, highlight what makes you the best candidate, and discuss why you want to work for the organization you are applying for. You should have a noncompany-specific version to use on LinkedIn. Early in your college career, you should make a good attempt at creating a well-planned video. Graphics and fancy multimedia techniques are not necessary, but as you near entering the job market, you may want to consider adding advance features. Early in your college career is a wonderful time to learn new things. You do not need fancy equipment. Most phones equipped with video will do the trick. I encourage you to experiment and take this opportunity to learn new things.

It might feel overwhelming to think about creating a video about yourself to use during job hunting. Most of us are not comfortable with seeing ourselves on video. This exercise will boost your confidence. The video is short, so that is an advantage. It video should include specific information, including an introduction, resume highlights, why you want to work in the specific field or industry, and a call to action. The introduction should consist of your name and some basic information about yourself and your objective in job hunting. You will want to include the industry and type of position you are looking for. After the introduction you will want to highlight your resume. This should include selecting a few experiences and accomplishments that help support and provide evidence of your story. Provide a clear statement explaining why you want to work in the industry. You might revisit various mission statement of companies in the industry and look for a common thread. If there is a common thread, work it in your rationale for why you want to work in the industry. Keep in mind organizations want employees who will help them deliver on their mission statement. The more you can convince prospective employers that you can add value to their company and play a role in delivering the mission, the more attractive you will be to them. Remember the goal of the video is to be persuasive. The last part of the video is to include a call to action. Give the viewer something to do, such as visit an electronic portfolio or social media. Be cautious about including personal contact information. Don't include phone numbers, unless you create a phone number using the internet or an app. Do not include your address. Don't forget you must be in the video; after all you are showcasing yourself. I recommend searching the internet for examples. As previously mentioned, YouTube has many real video resumes that were both successful and unsuccessful. See the New Tools for a New Generation box at the end of the chapter for a few examples.

Building a Portfolio of Evidence of Employability

The last item you should put time and effort in thinking about is a professional portfolio. The good news is you have already done some of the work of establishing a portfolio. A **portfolio** is a collection of examples of your work with the intent of demonstrating your skills and competencies. The best way to think of a portfolio is as proof and evidence to support the claims you made in your cover letter and resume. Be sure to keep track of writing samples, awards, presentations, and other forms of evidence of your skills and competencies. Many communication programs have portfolios built into the major. If not, don't let that stop you from taking the initiative to create one on your own. Once you have one created a portfolio, share it with a few faculty and your academic advisor for advice and first impressions. Go one step further, and ask faculty and other connections to recommend someone currently in your desired industry to review it and share first impressions. It is invaluable to receive feedback from those currently working in the industry. Not only will the industry professional give you priceless feedback, but they will see your initiative and how you respond to feedback. You will most likely be in the forefront of their mind when they learn of an opportunity connected with your career intentions. You might find a mentor through this experience; it is a tremendous opportunity. You may be wondering about some common items communication majors include in their portfolios. Weber State University's Department of Communication has links to several students' portfolios (https://www.weber.edu/Communication/ePortfolio.html). Monmouth College's Department of Communication Studies also has links to students' portfolios (https://department.monm.edu/cata/portfolios.htm). As mentioned earlier, portfolios may be hard copies or available online. It is more common these days to have an online portfolio; however, certain industries still require a hard copy. The arrangement of the items is key; you want to ensure the documents are well organized and easy to manage. The best way of using your portfolio is linking to it on your social media and including the URL on your resume and LinkedIn account. When you create business cards, add the URL or create QR codes

---

TOOLS FOR A NEW GENERATION

Here is a list of resources to watch and read. Each reinforces the topics presented in the chapter.

College Info Greek Episode 157 (2017): "How to Build a Good Relationship With Your Professor"

This podcast provides useful information for navigating the relationship you have with your faculty. Strong relationships bring rewards. Connecting with your faculty will promote interactions and put you in their awareness. When opportunities are available they will be more likely to share with you.

READ AT https://collegeinfogeek.com/how-to-build-relationship-with-professor/

(continued ...)

Dan Schwabel (2009): *Me 2.0: 4 Steps to Building Your Future*

This book shares meaningful recommendations for building a personal brand. Using tested tools will give you the competitive advantage when developing your career.

READ AT https://danschawbel.com/me-2-0/

Dorie Clark (2013): *Reinventing You*

This book provides tools for managing change and building your personal brand. At times the author focuses on changing jobs. Although this may seem like it does not apply to you, indeed you are transitioning from student to professional. Adapt what you read to match your personal situation.

READ AT https://dorieclark.com/reinventingyou/

Tom Peters (1997): *"The Brand Called You"*

This article is an oldie yet a goodie. Tom Peters is cited by many others. Peters translates branding principles successful companies use into personal branding strategies.

READ AT https://www.fastcompany.com/28905/brand-called-you

KEY TERMS

mission statement: A brief statement that describes why an organization exists, its purpose, and its overall goal. It is not uncommon for individual majors, clubs, and even special events in colleges to have a mission statement.

personal brand: An intentional effort to mold the perception of others, specifically prospective employers and colleagues, by showcasing skills and expertise that differentiates you from others (competitors). The goal of a personal brand is to raise your potential impact within your desired career industry.

portfolio: A collection of work that serves as evidence of skills and expertise. A portfolio might be a hard copy or electronic.

relational network mapping: A record of people you have worked with and experiences, milestones, turning points, and so on worth remembering.

video cover letter: A brief, no longer than 2-minute video that allows you address prospective employers, introducing them to your work experience and overall fit with the prospective job.

Part II

THE BUSINESS OF COMMUNICATION

CHAPTER 4

Aligning Your Goals

What were your first thoughts when you read the title of this chapter, aligning your goals? It is something that you have probably heard from parents, high school teachers, college faculty, advisor and so many more people. Most people don't start a venture thinking they are going to settle for less than the full experience. Instead, it is more common that you decided to attend college with a goal in mind. The goal may have been very specific, like working at your hometown news station, or a bit vague, like graduating with a job in the field of your major. Whatever the goal you had at the start of your college search and selection process, you should monitor it and revise it as necessary. Goals should not be static; rather, they should be dynamic and grow with you and your career journey.

SMART and SMARTE Goals

The best goals are **SMART goals**—**S**pecific, **M**easurable, **A**ttainable, **R**elevant, and **T**ime-based (Esposito, 2015). Each element of the SMART framework works together to create a goal that is carefully planned, clear, and trackable (see figure 4.1). It is valuable to understand how to set specific, measurable, attainable, relevant, and time-based goals. Too often faculty hear students state that their goal after graduation is to have a job after college. In reality this goal meets many of the elements of SMART goals; however, it may not the best goal to set. Why? The one element having a job after college does not contain is specificity. Having a job is measurable, attainable, and time-based. Is it relevant? It depends on how you define relevant. Having a job after college is not relevant, or may not be, to your college major or your career dreams. It is relevant, as a job will pay the bills and allow you to live independently from your parents. I suggest adding an **E** to SMART goals. The most effective goals should be elevating. The goals you set and achieve should elevate you to a new place in your career (and life). Having a job after college is not elevating. If you employed the **SMARTE goals** technique, you could refine the goal, so it is specific to your career intentions and one that would take you to the goal and surpass it. Be sure the goals you set are your own—not your parents', advisor's, or faculty's.

Specific goals are clear. There is no ambiguity in the goal statement. Start by writing a statement that reflects your goal. When you think about your career goal for when you graduate, what do you think of? Write it down. Now, make it more specific. To do this ask yourself what you want to accomplish, when you want to do accomplish it, and who else needs to be included. Finally, ask yourself why this is a goal. Answering these questions will help you write a specific goal. How is could this goal be measurable? How would you know if you achieved this goal? Next, determine if this goal is attainable. Do you have the necessary skills to reach your goal? If you do not have the goals, how can you obtain them? For a goal to be attainable, you will need to be motivated to work for it. What is your motivation for this goal? Are you willing to do the necessary work to achieve the goal in the time you stated? Is the goal relevant? Why are you setting the goal at this time in your life? Is it appropriate for the life stage you are in? Is the goal aligned with your overall career objectives? The goal needs to be trackable. What is the deadline? Is the deadline realistic? Lastly, how is the goal elevating you? Are you aiming too low with your goal? Does the goal add value to your life and career?

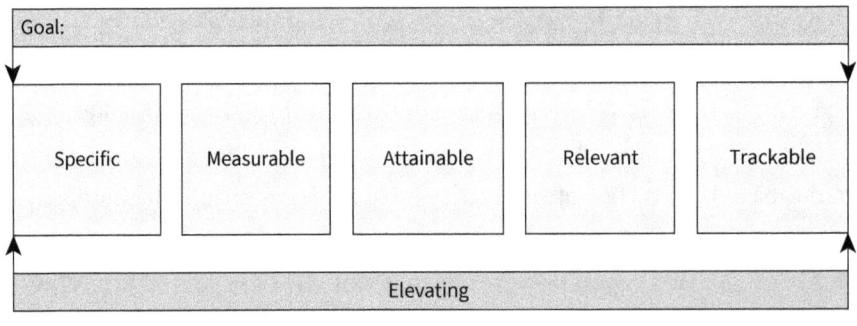

FIGURE 4.1   SMARTE Goals

SWOT Analysis

Now that you have thought about your goals and applied the SMARTE goal model to refining your goals, it is important to assess whether you have the correct goals. One helpful tool is the **SWOT analysis** (Graybeal, 2017). You might be familiar with SWOT; it is commonly used by business people. And if you are not familiar with it, chances are you are probably familiar with the four components. Using the SWOT you can examine a specific idea; in this case the idea is you! The four components are strengths, weaknesses, opportunities, and threats.

Corporate SWOTs

The SWOT is a technique for assessing the most important aspects of a business. It is used to examine the market and competition. The SWOT is usually a key part of a business plan. It is useful to look at three successful companies and review some of the factors in each one's SWOT analysis and consider how your personal SWOT might be similar.

COCA-COLA'S SWOT

Take the Coca-Cola Company for example. It is one of the largest companies in the world, with an iconic brand. Did you know that the Coca-Cola Company, like most successful companies, routinely use a SWOT tool? What do you think are some of the company's strengths? The company, for one, has many products across different categories. The Coca-Cola Company owns over 500 brands and offers 3,500 beverages in over 200 countries (Coca-Cola, n.d.). With this vast product line, the company has a large share of the soft drink industry. Another strength is its globally recognized brand. You might also consider their unique "secret" recipe for their drinks a strength. Coca-Cola sounds like a strong company; does it actually have weaknesses?

One of its weaknesses is its inability to keep stride with the health industry. Coca-Cola's reliance on sugar in its drink's may be viewed as a weakness, especially in health-conscious societies. The strength of the brand image may be viewed as a weakness, as it is challenging to break away from the image. For example, Coca-Cola has struggled gaining position in the health drink industry (Fahad, 2016). With such a stronghold on the soft drink industry and so many brands and products, are there any opportunities left for Coca-Cola? Of course! There are very few actual real competitors in the soft drink industry. Did you know Coca-Cola offers a version of its iconic drink with coffee in it or a Coca-Cola Energy drink? Coca-Cola has the opportunity to compete in the healthy drink industry with more alignment with the health trends. Also, like Pepsi, Coca-Cola could diversify into different industry, such as food. Pepsi Co. owns brands including Lays, Quaker Oats, and Doritos. What about threats? Other companies, especially those that offer a healthier alternative to Coca-Cola, can be seen as threats. Some of the company's competitors include Pepsi Co., Nestlé, and Dr. Pepper Snapple Group. Bad press is always a threat to a company, and Coca-Cola is no exception (Fahad, 2016). There have been many stories about Coca-Cola not being good for you (Felman, 2019). Over the years, the company has been the subject of human rights and racism stories.

Consider this discussion of Coca-Cola through the lens of the SWOT analysis. Can you see similarities between the factors in Coca Cola's analysis and what might be in your analysis? Consider your personal brand as a student and as a future member of your intended industry. Wouldn't it be a dream to have a strong personal brand for which you are globally known for being at the top of your field? How do you use the SWOT analysis to build your brand, as discussed in the previous chapter?

EXERCISE 4.1
Lessons From the Coca-Cola SWOT Analysis

Use the following SWOT analysis template to write what you can use from Coca-Cola in each component of the SWOT.

Strengths	Weaknesses
Coca-Cola's strength:	Coca-Cola's weakness:
My strength:	My weakness:
Opportunities	**Threats**
Coca-Cola's opportunity:	Coca-Cola's threat:
My opportunity:	My threat:

ZARA'S SWOT

Let's turn our attention to another company. Zara is one of the largest clothing brands in the world (Hanbury, 2018). The brand is owned by the Spanish company Inditex, which was founded in 1985. Zara is known for imitating fashion trends. When thinking about Zara's strengths their efficient operational processes, such as manufacturing, delivery, and logistics, rise the top of the industry. Zara has a very quick turnaround time from idea to manufacturing to delivery. This enables them to act when a new trend is established to create clothing. They can stay abreast of trends. Zara also is considered to have a competitive pricing structure. With over 2,000 stores Zara has a large global presence. Their parent company, Inditex, is a strong company and offers support and leadership for Zara. Like Coca-Cola, Zara is a strong global brand, but also like Coca-Cola, Zara has some weaknesses too.

Zara does not market or advertise. In current times in which brands have a large social media presence and following, Zara could get lost. The strength of having a quick turnaround time could be a weakness because there is a limited production of each clothing item (Shastri, 2022). Stores get a limited supply, and sizing is limited. Like Coca-Cola, Zara has been involved in scandals regarding child labor and paying under minimum wage.

Opportunities exist for Zara, like for most companies. There is a growing desire for reasonable high fashion. Fashion is consumable in that people get tired of trends and want to be able to stay on top of the changing trends. For example, during the height of the COVID-19 pandemic, people bought less pants and skirts and instead bought more business shirts that would look good on a video conferencing camera. Like most companies, Zara's threats include rising costs of raw materials and production. Additional threats would include increasing competition. Zara also has to monitor regulatory bodies for importing and exporting. Can you see similarities between the factors in Zara's analysis and what might be in your analysis? What about the ability to be agile? Do you think potential employers might value an employee who is agile in the workplace; if so, how do you become more agile and demonstrate your agility on your resume and in your interview?

EXERCISE 4.2
Lessons From the Zara SWOT Analysis

Use the following SWOT analysis template to write what you can use from Zara in each component of the SWOT. For optimal leaning, choose responses that differ from those in the Coca-Cola SWOT from Exercise 4.1.

(continued ...)

Strengths	Weaknesses
Zara's strength: My strength:	Zara's weakness: My weakness:
Opportunities	**Threats**
Zara's opportunity: My opportunity:	Zara's threat: My threat:

APPLE'S SWOT

A final example of a company's SWOT analysis to consider and reflect on is Apple. Do you think a mega successful company like Apple uses the SWOT analysis? Certainly. Consider Apple's strength. Did you say innovation? What sets Apple from many of their competitors is their ability to innovate in a manner that makes their products sought after, even long before they hit the marketplace (Dudovskiy, 2021).

Apple, like all companies, has weaknesses. A key weakness is the price point of their products. The higher price makes them less attainable for lower socioeconomic brackets. With the demand for mobile phones only increasing over time, Apple has opportunities to continue to innovate the mobile phone market and computer market. What threats does Apple face? Successful businesses can be threatened by copycats and new players in the marketplace. The technology industry is a very competitive space that is equally dynamic. What similarities are there between factors in Apple's analysis and your personal SWOT? Similar to Coca-Cola, Apple is a brand that is recognized for being a global industry leader. Apple's place in the marketplace is based on its ability to innovate (Jurevicius, 2021). You might consider how you can you demonstrate your ability to be a forward thinker to your prospective employer. What must you do to keep ahead of trends and anticipate changes in your prospective industry?

EXERCISE 4.3
Lessons From the Apple SWOT Analysis

Use the following SWOT analysis template to write what you can use from Apple in each component of the SWOT. For optimal learning, choose responses that differ from those in the Coca-Cola and Zara SWOT in the previous exercises.

Strengths	Weaknesses
Apple's strength:	Apple's weakness:
My strength:	My weakness:

Opportunities	Threats
Apple's opportunity:	Apple's threat:
My opportunity:	My threat:

Individual SWOTs

The SWOT analysis is a useful tool to examine, on an individual level, how to best prepare for the job market through professional development. In the previous exercises you started to write your own SWOT analysis. You used mini examples of businesses to get a sense of what your strengths, weaknesses, opportunities, and threats were as you prepare for the job market upon graduation.

Let's switch gears a bit and look at stories of four undergraduate students who took different approaches to their college experience yet all graduated within four years. Some were clearly successful in graduating with a job that aligned with their major and career intention. Others were less successful. It is common to hear faculty tell students that their destiny for the future lies in their own hands. Each college experience is analyzed with the strategy used by the student in mind and presents questions for reflection and application to your college experience. The stories presented here are inspired by real students and their college experiences; however, details have been changed as not to reveal students' identities. You will have the chance to do a mini SWOT analysis for each student in a story. After the four case studies you will have a chance to do a full and complete SWOT analysis to use as you develop professionally throughout your college years. The case studies that follow introduce four college students: Rachel, Marco, Tyrone, and Mai.

RACHEL'S SWOT ANALYSIS

Meet Rachel, who started college as a biology major. After her first year, she decided to change her major to communication. During her first year, she struggled to manage the course load of two biology classes with other general electives. She spoke with family members and her advisor and realized some of the assignments she enjoyed the most were those where she worked with others on group projects and when she gave presentations. She was not like many first year students, as Rachel really enjoyed talking in class. She rushed a Greek organization and quickly became identified as someone with leadership potential. In her second year, Rachel won the election to be the communication director of her sorority. She started taking more communication courses in the spring of her sophomore year. Faculty started relying on her as someone they could depend on. Rachel was always ready to help—so much so that in her sophomore year she started a fundraiser to help families impacted by a devastating hurricane. She identified how she could fundraise and how to include others. Her efforts were a great success. She raised over $72,000 to donate to a local charity assisting impacted families.

Not everything came easily to Rachel. She feared one course in particular: research methods. She decided early on that she would attack the class from the start. She did not wait until her grade was suffering to engage with a tutor. She recommended to the teaching faculty that a formal teaching assistant be used, a student who had successfully earned an A in the class, to hold regular study sessions. Rachel was dedicated to attending each one. Later in her junior year she was approached by a faculty member to start a student organization. Rachel saw this as a great opportunity. Not only would it be fun and interesting, she knew it would look great on a resume and provide a possible example to use in an interview. Rachel worked with the faculty to plan meetings and the first big event. The faculty asked Rachel, as the organization's president, to moderate the panel event. The event was postponed but finally took place in Rachel's senior year. Rachel was a bit nervous but jumped in with both feet. She always liked a challenge. In her role as moderator she sent emails to all the panelists and helped create the structure for the panel discussion and event. After the event was over, Rachel was pleased with her work.

Fast forward a couple of months, and Rachel found a message in her LinkedIn account from one of the panelists. It turned out the panelist was impressed by Rachel and wanted to consider her for a job. Over the next few weeks, the woman shared another opportunity she thought Rachel would be great for, even though she really wanted to be the one to hire Rachel. Rachel interviewed for both jobs but decided to accept the first one—the one the panelist offered her. Rachel and her academic advisor, as well as the advisor for the new student organization, met throughout this process. Rachel found it helpful to have someone who was familiar with the industry, companies, and managers to process the offers. Three weeks before graduation Rachel was fully employed. Her job was in the field of communication. She felt excited to be using the information she learned in her major in a job. She is confident her manager will be a great mentor and that the position has growth potential for the future.

EXERCISE 4.4
Lessons From Rachel's SWOT Analysis

Using information provided in the case study of Rachel's college experience complete a brief SWOT analysis. Keep in mind the goal is to recognize each component of the SWOT and continue reflecting on your experience.

Strengths	Weaknesses

Opportunities	Threats

Questions

1. After completing Rachel's SWOT, what advice would you give her?
2. Did she miss any opportunities, in your opinion, for making the most of your college experience?
3. How are you similar to Rachel? How are you different?
4. What can you learn or take away from Rachel's approach to college?

MARCO'S SWOT ANALYSIS

Meet Marco, who started and finished college as a communication major with a political science minor. Marco went to college on the other side of the country from where he lived with his family. He always wanted to be a lawyer. He decided that a communciation degree would prepare him for law school. Marco was a talented althete. He was on paritial scholarship as a member of the cross coutnry team. He was dedicated to his team and never complained about the early 5:00 a.m. practice before classes. Marco was always a student faculty could depend on. He was prepared for class, well-organized, and participated in each class meeting. At least once a semester, Marco made an appointment with each of his faculty to discuss classes and his future plans. It was not uncommon to see Marco drop in during office hours to have an information conversation with a faculty member. He valued the access he had to his faculty members. He once asked a communication faculty to review his resume and provide pointers. When the faculty offered suggestions and referred him to the university career services, Marco made an appointment and followed up with the faculty.

In his sophmore, Marco was recommended for a scholarship. This allowed him to participate in the republican conventions for presidency. He shadowed journalists during the covention and reflected on this experience with his academic advisor. Marco served as the president of the communicaiton club and worked to invite guest speakers to share with students their career journey. Marco really valued meeting with industry professionals. In his junior year, Marco was invited by one of his faculty to join him at the National Communication Association's annual convention. She introduced him to faculty at other universities, and he attended panel sessions. This experience really got him thinking about the next step. In his senior year, Marco won the president's award for the most outstanding athlete. Marco decided his road to law school would include a detour to graduate school to earn a master's degree in communication and advocacy. He often spoke with his advisor for advice; she really become a mentor to him. Once he graduated with his bachelor's degree in communication, he felt ready for graduate school. This two-year period would provide him the additional education that directly related to being an effective lawyer. Plus, he would gain futher public speaking practice as a gradaute teaching assistant while in graduate school. Marco was feeling good about his future.

EXERCISE 4.5
Lessons from Marco's SWOT Analysis

Using information provided in the case study of Marco's college experience complete a brief SWOT analysis. Keep in mind the goal is to recognize each component of the SWOT and continue reflecting on your experience.

Strengths	Weaknesses
Opportunities	**Threats**

Questions

1. After completing Marco's SWOT, what advice would you give him?
2. Did he miss any opportunities, in your opinion, for making the most of your college experience?
3. How are you similar to Marco? How are you different?
4. What can you learn or take away from Marco's approach to college?

TYRONE'S SWOT ANALYSIS

Meet Tyrone, who started college as an undecided major. He spent his first two years taking his general education class. He noticed that he scored usually high on writing assignments, and his instructors commented on his writing skills. He was not sure what to do with this interest. One day in the fall of his sophomore year, one of his instructors suggested he consider public relations as a major. He made an appointment with an advisor and decided to declare his major as public relations. He spent the next two years taking communication classes, and he did fairly in his classes.

Tyrone had a difficult time staying motivated. It was not unusual for him to be late in submitting assignment or missing a submission altogether. In one class he forgot to complete the take-home midterm exam. It was not until two weeks that he approached the faculty confessing he completely forgot about the midterm. The faculty was not sympathetic to Tyrone's forgetfulness, although he offered a take-home research paper as an alternative. The faculty told Tyrone they would grade the research paper as the midterm, but they wanted him to then take the feedback and review the paper to submit to the academic excellence conference that university holds each spring. Tyrone thanked his faculty and promised to do a solid job on the research paper. The agreed-upon deadline came and passed, with Tyrone not submitting the paper.

Tyrone was great at participating in class. He was always engaged in the discussions, and he was not shy about participating. Tyrone was living his best life while at college. He was a member of a fraternity, which he really enjoyed. He also played intramural sports, such as soccer and basketball. Graduation approached quickly for Tyrone. During the months leading up to graduation he wondered where the time went. He started reviewing his portfolio, which he was required to have for his major. All of his courses had one assignment that was added to the portfolio. As he reviewed the work he realized he did not take full advantage of the feedback he received on the assignments. Students received feedback in all their classes and then had the opportunity in a senior capstone class to strengthen the entire portfolio by addressing previous feedback on assignments. Tyrone realized he did not put much effort in editing and strengthening the assignments.

Still, Tyrone thought he was prepared for the job market; after all, he had a college degree. About two weeks before graduation, Tyrone started applying for jobs. To his surprise it was hard. Finding open positions that did not require years of experience was difficult. Applications were long and took endless hours to complete and submit. After graduation he received an email he had received a million times before from the university's career services, but because his job search was so challenging, this time, he opened and read the email. It was an invitation for new graduates to attend a networking event. Tyrone realized this is something he should have been doing all along. He attended the session and got good advice. He updated his resume and applied to more jobs. It took Tyrone a few months before he landed a full-time job. It was not really in his field, but he felt confident with the additional experience he would find a public relations job.

EXERCISE 4.6
Lessons From Tyrone's SWOT Analysis

Using information provided in the case study of Tyrone's college experience complete a brief SWOT analysis. Keep in mind the goal is to recognize each component of the SWOT and continue reflecting on your experience.

Strengths	Weaknesses

(continued ...)

Opportunities	Threats

Questions

1. After completing Tyrone's SWOT, what advice would you give him?
2. Did he miss any opportunities, in your opinion, for making the most of your college experience?
3. How are you similar to Tyrone? How are you different?
4. What can you learn or take away from Tyrone's approach to college?

MAI'S SWOT ANALYSIS

Meet Mai, who was a digital communication major at her local state university. Mai was well liked by faculty. She was quiet and did not participate much during classes, though she did make a habit of speaking with some of her communication faculty during office hours. He mother told her that building relationships is an important part of college. Mai was good about remembering that point.

Mai was not really involved during her first two years of college. She was a commuter and felt a bit disconnected to the campus. She worked part-time at a design company. She did not have much responsibility for actual design, but it was useful to see the everyday work of a graphic designer. The summer between her sophomore year and junior year, Mai made some changes. She strategized how she could get more out of college, especially when working on projects. She completed her resume and used it as a document to help create goals. When she returned to class a semester later, the faculty noticed the change in Mai and gave her positive feedback. Hearing the faculty recognize the hard work she put in over the summer made all the difference to Mai. She felt empowered. She finished her college years strong, applied to graduate school, and was accepted.

In the early years after graduating, she worked as a teacher and completed a master's degree. Working with students of a lower socioeconomic status, social issues started to become in her awareness. She decided to become a lawyer and was accepted to school. Years after she graduated from her undergraduate degree she reached back to the faculty and told them how much the words acknowledging her change in attitude and work made all the difference to her and her choices after graduation.

EXERCISE 4.7

Lessons From Mai's SWOT Analysis

Using information provided in the case study of Mai's college experience complete a brief SWOT analysis. Keep in mind the goal is to recognize each component of the SWOT and continue reflecting on your experience.

Strengths	Weaknesses

(continued ...)

Opportunities	Threats

Questions

1. After completing Mai's SWOT, what advice would you give her?
2. Did she miss any opportunities, in your opinion, for making the most of your college experience?
3. How are you similar to Mai? How are you different?
4. What can you learn or take away from Mai's approach to college?

Personal SWOT

Your college experience has to be more than getting a piece of paper. A piece of paper does not transform your life; experiences do! It is important to share ideas throughout your college experiences, both inside the classroom and outside. Share stories. Stories are impactful in creating your reality. Listen and be mindful of the stories others tell. Many stories are inspirational or tell of lessons learned. Reap the benefit of others' experiences and career journeys. Share moments. Get involved, and become part of your university, department, and major. Get feedback. Read the feedback on all your assignments. Determine your weaknesses as well as strengths. Keep a record, mapping patterns. If there is a pattern, I promise it will not suddenly disappear. Patterns are the results of consistent, repetitive behaviors. If patterns are positive, then take comfort they will most likely be enduring. Learn from these patterns. How might these patterns be related to a career or resume items? Keep a keen eye on negative patterns. These patterns should reveal important information about your weakness and areas you might want to work to improve. It will be especially important to determine the best way to turn your weaknesses or gaps in skills into resume-worthy experience. As we have discussed in this chapter, the SWOT analysis will help you examine the patterns of your skills, as revealed in the feedback received on assignments.

Competition for jobs is fierce. Recent statistics show just how competitive the job market is, especially for recent graduates. According to the May 2021 website article "What to Become," recent research shows there have been 10 million jobs lost in the United States since the pandemic, and 7.3 million Americans are getting unemployment benefits (Jacimovic, 2021). Additionally, there is an average of 250 resumes received per job opening, with only 2% of applicants getting an interview. It takes companies an average of 42 days to hire an applicant. Jacimovic (2021) asserts that 80% of jobs are not posted online. Making the most of your college years is important to have a competitive advantage upon graduation.

There are many different things you could do to make the most of your college experiences. Most of these things fall into several categories. Firstly, be social; it is important that you start meeting all types of people while in college. Of course, you want to make friends, but you also want to build professional relationships with faculty and staff. It might not cross your mind to meet locals. Locals are great to connect with because they will give you insight into the local community and job opportunities. You also never know who people know. It could be that the person at the coffee shop owns a small business and needs help with a communication plan or some graphic design work.

Secondly, create your own luck. You will often hear people describe someone else's success as luck. Do not be fooled into thinking this is always the case. Luck can be engineered. Be in places around campus and the local community where you have greater chances to meet new people and see new things. Volunteer. Make opportunities rather than waiting for opportunities to happen. One thing I know is that waiting for opportunities is on someone else's timeline. Create your own timeline, and then seek out the available opportunities. Read. Truly, this is important. You might be thinking you already spend a great amount of time reading. What are you reading? Are you reading *Fortune Magazine* or *Forbes*? I know you are not a business major, but it is still important to learn about business. Business is the environment that will provide you with a job.

There is a great scene from the 1988 movie *Working Girl*, staring Melanie Griffith, which focuses on the character Tess trying to get ahead in her job. Tess is working on her college degree in business and working as a stockbroker's secretary. She has a habit of reading and keeping up with all the local business news. When she read information in the newspaper she was able to pitch an idea to the boss while bumping into him in the elevator. He inquired how she put the pieces of the pitch together all from community news. This scene depicts how important and relevant it is to be well-read in business, especially in your industry.

As a final note, truly approach your college years as a time when anything is possible. Dream big, but be ready to back up the dream with hard work. Believe anything is possible and that it could happen to you. College years are a time you get to reinvent yourself, again and again. Use this time to be strategic about what you learn about yourself and your desired industry.

EXERCISE 4.8
Personal SWOT Analysis

Use the information in the chapter to complete your own SWOT analysis. I recommend you revisit your SWOT once a semester as you add more skills and discover new opportunities.

Strengths	Weaknesses
Opportunities	**Threats**

SPOTLIGHT ON COMMUNICATION
Communication Strategy

Much has been written about strategic communication. Organizational communication researchers have examined how an organization can communicate to achieve specific objectives. Strategic communication is a way of persuading other people to accept your ideas toward accomplishing a goal. Strategic communication is often connected to public relations. We know that a communication strategy must contain goals, a target or intended audience, a plan, and identified channels. Consider how the SWOT analysis tool aligns with building a strategy. When completing a personal SWOT, you must examine the context, or why you are conducting the analysis. Unlike organizational communication strategy your target or intended audience is not employees or other stakeholders but your desired career industry. You will need to take a deep look into yourself to see what the industry may view as a weakness. You will also need to understand the industry to recognize opportunities and threats. The purpose of the SWOT is collecting information, so you can develop a solid plan of action and develop your SMARTE goals into reality. By identifying opportunities you can identify what means (or channels) you will use to develop your weaknesses and capitalize on your strengths.

Debriefing

When you have completed your personal SWOT, examine each of the four areas. Look at the strengths you have listed, and determine what evidence you have to demonstrate the strengths. Future employers will ask for evidence of strengths. Do you have an item on your resume that connects to the strength? Do you have work in your portfolio? Do you have a professional who could write a letter of recommendation ensure your skills? Use the following space to capture notes about evidence of strengths:

_____
_____
_____
_____

Next, examine your weaknesses, and think about how you can turn each into a strength. Ideally, your weaknesses will provide a roadmap of activities you need to seek out during your college years. Look over the course curriculum for your major, and identify where you may work on some of your weaknesses. For example, you may not know anything about social media except as a user. You see that your university offers a course is social media writing and one on social media marketing. You may see if one of these courses could fit into your schedule. Use the following space to start planning ways to strengthen your weaknesses while gaining new (or improved) competency:

_____
_____
_____
_____

Once you have identified and reflected on both your strengths and weaknesses, consider opportunities you have or could have to showcase your strengths (and, as previously discussed, work on weaknesses). Think about class projects, off-campus jobs, internships, projects, student academic conferences, clubs, leadership positions, and so on. Use the following space to capture your ideas:

_____
_____
_____
_____

Be mindful that we live in an ever-changing world. Business is more global than ever, and specific social issues have risen to the attention of our organizations. The COVID-19 pandemic has had an effect on most areas of society, including the workforce. As you examine your goals and the threats you identified, reflect on how your degree is preparing you for the future of your industry, not just for the immediate time. Use the following space to brainstorm potential changes in the industry in the future. Also, consider how agile you are at adapting as the industry changes:

_____
_____
_____
_____

TOOLS FOR ALIGNING YOUR GOALS

Here is a list of resources to watch and read. Each reinforces the topics presented in the chapter.

Indeed Editorial Team (2021): "How to Write SMART Goals (With Examples)"

If you need additional help identifying and writing SMART goals, consult the following website. It has additional examples for writing SMART goals.

READ AT https://www.indeed.com/career-advice/career-development/how-to-write-smart-goals

Dominika Cechova (2019): "20 Examples of SMART Goals for Employees"

The following website provides a useful template employees can use to set SMART goals. As a student you can begin to use this template to help prepare for the workforce.

READ AT https://www.peoplegoal.com/blog/examples-of-smart-goals-for-employees

Skills You Need (n.d.): "Personal SWOT Analysis"

Consult the following website for more information and coaching on using the SWOT analysis tool to better position yourself for the job market.

READ AT https://www.skillsyouneed.com/ps/personal-swot-analysis.html

KEY TERMS

SMART goals: Goals that are specific, measurable, attainable, relevant and time-based.

SMARTE goals: An extension of SMART goals. The most effective goals should be elevating. The goals you set and achieve should elevate you to a new place in your career (and in life).

SWOT analysis: A business tool that helps analyze a specific idea, organization, situation, etc. SWOT stands for examining four components of a specific idea. The four components are strengths, weaknesses, opportunities, and threats.

CREDITS

IMG 4.1: Copyright © 2020 Depositphotos/HayDmitriy.
IMG 4.2: Copyright © 2021 Pexels/RODNAE Productions.
IMG 4.3: Copyright © 2021 Pexels/Michael Burrows.
IMG 4.4: Copyright © 2020 Pexels/Zen Chung.
IMG 4.5: Copyright © 2011 Depositphotos/PixelsAway.

CHAPTER 5

Choosing a Career in Communication

Do you remember when you started thinking about going or returning to college? You most likely explored your options. Perhaps you considered local universities and colleges, then maybe out of state, and then maybe online. You likely compared cost of attendance, options for financial assistance, flexibility, and the timeline for completing your degree. In addition, you looked at the classes you would be enrolling in for the specific degree. Choosing a college consisted of looking at many different variables. You might have applied aspects of a SWOT analysis discussed in the previous chapter. You examined advantages (strengths), disadvantages (weaknesses), opportunities, and threats (e.g., not getting accepted).

Choosing a career and creating a path to that career is similar to choosing a college. There are many variables that contribute to your interest in a specific career. In this chapter you will be on a guided tour of elements that contribute to your search and, ultimately, choice of a career upon graduation. It is a great opportunity think about your career choices and to be future focused.

Carter: A Case Study

Meet Carter, who has always been well liked by his teachers. He is a good student but frankly never put too much effort into his high school classes. Carter was active in high school; he acted in the annual student theatre production. One of the things that drew him to acting was the interaction with the audience. He learned after his first play that he loved the response from the audience. He soon found himself craving that type of rush. He found a great part-time job working at the local amusement park as one of the characters. Although Carter did not like how hot the costume was, he adored interacting with children and adults and taking on this larger-than-life personality.

In his senior year, Carter applied to several colleges and universities. Most of them were not too far from home. When people asked him about where he wanted to go, he was never sure what to say. The truth is it was hard for him to imagine himself at any particular college because he did not know what he wanted to major in. As acceptance letters arrived, he started feeling stress about not having a specific major in mind. One day before Christmas, one of Carter's teachers spoke to the class about finding one's passion in life and making a career of that passion. It really got Carter thinking about the future. What was he passionate about? After much reflection, Carter realized he wanted to interact with people each and every day. He did not see himself sitting behind a desk each day for the rest of his life. He wanted to create joy for others. In a way he wanted to put on a show for others.

Prior to graduation, Carter committed to a local university with a thriving theatre department. He was confident he had a plan for the future. Come fall, he enrolled in his first semester of college. His course load included the typical general education courses and one theatre class. He was so psyched about his introduction to acting class. He was certain he was living his dream.

The fall semester did not go as planned for Carter. He struggled in some of his classes, and it was easy to interact with his new friends and be social on campus. His introduction to acting class was fun, and he felt he was learning a lot of new things. He, unfortunately, did not get selected for a role in the fall play. He was bummed. One day on the way to class he saw a flyer hanging in the student union for the communication club. He had never given communication much thought. He actually wasn't sure what the major was about. He considered himself a great communicator and a people person; after all he was well liked by his teachers and had lots of friends. Something about the flyer caught his attention, and he decided to attend the membership recruitment meeting.

At this meeting he learned what the major of communication was all about. He was amazed to hear there was so much diversity across communication careers. Later in the fall when it was time to register for spring classes, Carter decided to sign up for the Introduction to Communication class. He was in seeing what this class and major was really about. It sounded so promising.

Come spring, Carter started his new courses. He learned throughout the semester that communication provided the opportunity to work with people and do so much more. He saw himself as a communication major. He took several communication classes over the following semesters. By his junior year he started becoming stressed, just like when he was in high school. He wasn't sure about applying for jobs for after graduation. What could he do with a communication degree after graduation? Would he be able to get a job? Would he make enough money to move out of his parents' house? All these thoughts overwhelmed Carter. He decided to reach out to his academic advisor.

During a meeting with his advisor in his junior year, Carter was encouraged to take an internship with the local chamber of commerce. At first this did not excite Carter. He did not even really know what a chamber of commerce did. He really respected his advisor, so he decided to follow the advice. Throughout the internship he learned so much about the local community and the businesses that operated there. He was able to participate in monthly chamber breakfasts, and there was even a cool breakfast that honored students of the month from the local schools. His site supervisor was great at introducing him to local business owners and managers. He really felt lucky to have this opportunity to build his network. One breakfast he sat next to the director of a nonprofit who provided safe after school programs for children living in foster care. Carter never thought about foster care children, but after speaking to the director, he became more interested in the mission of the nonprofit. Before Christmas in his junior year, he accepted a second internship—this time with the nonprofit. Carter spent the entire spring semester interning at the nonprofit. He learned so much about the foster care system and the needs of the children. Also, he realized that his passion for creating joy for others was easily used in this internship. He enjoyed going to the site to work. The director assigned him to one of the social media directors. He learned so much about social media. Carter began to connect the dots and considered a career in social media. Fortunately, Carter was able to get a part-time summer job managing the social media for a local pet store. He created fun posts and even designed a contest in which customers could submit photos of their pets for a chance at a fun prize pack of pet toys and treats. Who knew people loved sharing photos of their silly pets. Come his senior year, Carter realized he needed to take more classes on social media and even enrolled in social media marketing and web analytics classes.

His senior year consisted of taking classes and working part-time. He also volunteered at a nearby senior-living facility, where he helped the residents use email and social media to stay in touch with family and friends. The residents made him laugh and appreciate that he could share his skills with them. They also told some great stories about their childhood and families.

The spring semester of his final year in college came, and Carter started applying to many different jobs. Comparing his list of job applications with his friends' lists, he was happy that his communication major provided so much breadth, resulting in many career options.

Carter's story emphasizes some of the benefits of having communication as your major. Communication is the foundation of most things in life. Employers like communication majors because they know students have been instructed on effective verbal skills, both written and oral. There is a sense that communication students work well with other through collaboration. Additionally, communication majors can build both relationships and effective messages. As you work toward your bachelor's degree in communication, it is an exciting time to consider what life in your communication-based career may look like.

EXERCISE 5.1
Using the Occupational Outlook Handbook

Table 5.1 shows several different jobs Carter applied to in his senior year or later in his career. To gain an insight into Carter's career path read through the **occupational outlook handbook** descriptions for each position. Use the link to watch a video with a description of each job and listen to a person speak about the job who employed in that position. After watching the videos and reading the occupational outlook information, consider whether any of Carter's jobs interest you, and make a note why or why not. Take time to examine the occupational outlook for other positions you might be interested in exploring. Make notes for your future reference.

TABLE 5.1 **Job Outlooks and Descriptions**

Career	Link to Occupational Outlook	Link to Professional Describing the Job
Community Outreach Coordinator	[QR code]	[QR code]
Experiential Marketer	[QR code]	[QR code]

(continued ...)

Social Media Manager		
Community Events Coordinator (Public Relations)		

What I liked about jobs Carter held:

_____
_____
_____

What I did not like about jobs Carter held:

_____
_____
_____

Notes on the occupational outlook handbooks:

_____
_____
_____
_____

After viewing the occupational outlook page for each of the examples and viewing the video of a professional talking about their job, you should have a clearer idea of the opportunities available to communication majors. I often tell students that if you can dream it you can achieve it with a background in communication. As demonstrated by the story of Carter, seeking the guidance of both faculty and professionals is extremely important. Also, it is vital that you begin building your resume. You need to complete internship(s) and hold part-time jobs. If your schedule does not permit working, try volunteering. Your resume will tell the story of not only what you accomplished over the past few years, but it also serves as the vehicle that helps your interviewer or potential employer imagine your possibilities.

Advantages of a Communication Degree

The communication major provides students with great breadth of knowledge and experience as well as the opportunity to increase depth through minors, double majors, specializations or tracks, class projects or your portfolio, and internships. Students have many options upon graduation for jobs and career paths. It is important to use your breadth of experience as an advantage while focusing your skills and talents in a specific career path. Grand Canyon University (2020) identified three advantages of a communication degree. The advantages include being allowed to be creative in your work, having the ability to work in diverse fields, and having the option of many different roles and positions. The National Communication Association (2022) asserts that a communication degree allows students to be valued, get hired, and make a difference in the world. Communication majors are trained to understand the importance of communication and can transfer these skills to diverse industries and positions.

> **SPOTLIGHT ON COMMUNICATION**
> **Organizational Culture**
>
> Organizations are considered to have a unique culture. One might think about **organizational culture** as a complex recipe. Together, the individual ingredients are prepared and cooked in a specific manner, resulting in the unique dish. As you know, not everyone has the same tastes for food. What you like might be unappetizing to another person. Some dishes might even make you sick. Much is the same with an organizations' culture. Each organization has a unique personality. When entering the job market it is important to consider what culture or personality best suits you. One organization may be a better match to your values and interests as well as your approach to work.
>
> Organizational culture refers to shared assumptions, values, and beliefs of employees. Organizational culture is considered an important variable that strengthens an organization or weakens it. Think for a moment of what you know about Google. Google's organizational culture has been written and talked about for years. Search YouTube and watch any of the many videos on culture inside of Google. Now read Ross Brooks's article, "Workplace Spotlight: What Google Gets Right about Company Culture," (Brooks, 2018).
>
> Organizational culture, according to Schein (1990), exists on three interrelated levels: assumptions, values, and artifacts. **Assumptions** are the deepest level and refer to beliefs about reality. **Values**, as mentioned in this chapter, are principles or standards. The most directly observable features of culture are artifacts. **Artifacts** may include how the office space is organization, photos that may be displayed in employee offices, and
>
> (continued ...)

music playing in the office. Together, the three create distinct organizational cultures. The research suggests there are several basic types of cultures:

- **Innovative cultures** value being creative and appropriating work in different, even nontraditional, ways. For example, 3M has a 15% rule that allows any employee who has an intriguing idea to spend 15% of their work week developing their idea. Innovative cultures invest in creativity (Stoll, 2020).
- **Aggressive cultures** value competitiveness and outperforming the competition. Aggressive cultures invest in being profitable and top in their industry.
- **Outcome-oriented cultures** place importance on achievement, results, and action. Organizations with outcome-oriented cultures usually reward employees when short-term and long-term goals are achieved.
- **Stable cultures** value consistency. Additionally, stable cultures are usually rule governed and predictable. The U.S. military could be viewed as a stable culture.
- **People-oriented cultures** value treating people with dignity. These type of organizations tend to be supportive and emphasize respect.
- **Team-oriented cultures** emphasize working together as a team. Work is often done through cooperation among employees. Many of the processes within the organizations are done by teams.
- **Detailed-oriented cultures** value attention to even the smallest detail. There is value in performing at a high level through the attention to details.

Table 5.2 provides some examples of organizations for each of the types of cultures. Understanding different types of cultures helps you recognize which ones are the best fit for how you approach work.

TABLE 5.2 **Types of Cultures**

Cultures	Example Companies
Innovative cultures	W. L. Gore & Associates; 3M
Aggressive cultures	Microsoft; Uber; Amazon
Outcome-oriented cultures	Best Buy; Netflix
Stable cultures	Kraft Foods; Coca-Cola Co.
People-oriented cultures	Starbucks; Great Little Box Company; Warby Parker
Team-oriented cultures	Southwest Airlines; Bento's; Blackbaud
Detail-oriented cultures	Ritz Carlton Hotels; Four Season Hotels

You can apply the theory of organizational culture to developing your career path. As you are researching different industries, organizations, and jobs, you should be evaluating different aspects of the organizations' culture. You may do this by conducting an informal organizational culture assessment. As you are considering different organizations for future employment you are perfectly situated to do an impartial assessment. There are different ways to complete a cultural assessment. It is best if you have access to the organization and its employees.

INTERVIEWS AT AN ORGANIZATION

There are several important strategies you can employ during an interview that takes place at the organization you are interviewing for:

- Examine how employees interact with one another, including leadership.
- Look for displays of emotions. Emotions can tell a lot about a person's satisfaction. Do people seem engaged, happy, friendly, or withdrawn?
- Observe the objects employees surround themselves with. Do you see family photos? Announcements for events, such as picnics, birthday celebrations, etc.? Is the space sterile? Do employees seem to make their workspaces their own?
- If you have the ability to walk around, observe how the space is used. Where are the offices? Where are the common and gathering spaces?

During the interview is an appropriate time to learn even more about the culture. It is a time to ask questions, so you can assess aspects of the culture important to you. Following are some questions that might be helpful during an interview:

- What is the typical starting and ending time?
- What do you like most about working here?
- What were some traits or characteristics of the person who held this position that made them successful or unsuccessful?
- What makes this company different from others?
- Is there anything you would like to change about this department (or company) in the near future?

BEFORE AND AFTER AN INTERVIEW

There are several important strategies you can employ prior to and after an interview:

- Look online for any forums, review sites, or social media. How do employees talk about the company?
- Look for articles, stories, and videos that provide a view of employee job satisfaction. How happy are employees? Is there a sense of loyalty and trust among the employees? Is there low turnover of employees? There are several websites that track turnover and employee satisfaction. Some popular ones are Glassdoor and Fortune's rankings.
- Look for information on the company's website that talks about benefits and an approach to work that might hint at the work–life balance. For example, you might notice that company has many services at its campus, such as dry cleaning, a bank, a marketplace, a daycare, a gym, and similar services. You might be excited and consider all the perks a great advantage. Or you may wonder if the employees are overworked and have no time to complete these tasks outside of work. On the other hand, you might find the daycare to be a great perk and one that will save you money and time. You could see it as the company's investment in the employee and their family.
- Look for stories about recent projects the company completed. Do these stories mention a collaborative approach to work?
- Read the past few annual reports, if available. You can learn a lot about a company from the annual report. Keep in mind this report is written for stakeholders. You should be able to assess the company's productivity. As someone who is interested in practicing communication-related jobs it will be imperative to demonstrate that you understand how communication jobs function with other business processes.

- Read articles about the organization's leadership. What is that person's leadership style? Do you like what you read about the person? Does it match your style of followership?

Organizational culture theory can be a useful tool in determining whether or not an organization is matches your idea of work. Before entering the job market spend time reading business websites and magazines to learn about companies and how they conduct business. You will find that this knowledge will help you navigate the uncertainty of the job market but also impress future interviewers.

TOOLS FOR LEARNING ABOUT CAREERS IN COMMUNICATION

Here is a list of resources to watch and read. Each reinforces the topics presented in the chapter.

Kerry Schofield (2016): "Culture Fit in the Workplace"

READ AT https://www.linkedin.com/pulse/culture-fit-workplace-what-why-its-important-samar-birwadker

Kelci Lynn Lucier (2020): "16 Careers for Communications Majors"

READ AT https://www.thoughtco.com/careers-for-communications-majors-793111

Chartered Management Institute (2015): "Understanding Organisational Culture"

READ AT https://www.managers.org.uk/~/media/Files/PDF/Checklists/CHK-232-Understanding-organisational-culture.pdf

KEY TERMS

aggressive culture: Aggressive organizational cultures thrive on a spirit of competitiveness and outperforming others.

artifacts: Artifacts are objects or messages that reflect elements of an organization. These may be verbal or nonverbal.

assumptions: Assumptions are part of an organizational culture and refers to the deepest level representing beliefs about reality.

detail-oriented culture: Detail-oriented organizational cultures are characterized as having a competitive advantage over other organizational because of their attention to precision and details.

innovative culture: Innovative cultures are characterized by being flexible, adaptable, and experimenting.

occupational outlook handbook: A publication of the U.S Department of Labor's Bureau of Labor Statistics that is a collection of information about different occupations. The descriptions of the occupations include the nature of work, working conditions, training and education, earnings and job outlook.

organizational culture: Organization culture refers to shared assumptions, values, and beliefs of employees.

outcome-oriented culture: Outcome-oriented cultures place priority on results and achievements. This type of organization is often very dynamic and may have high turn-around of employees.

people-oriented culture: People-oriented organizational cultures ascribe to a human relations model of management which places value on fairness, supportiveness, and respecting individual rights as priorities.

stable culture: Stable organizational cultures are characterized by being predictable and rule-governed. There tends to high several layers in the hierarchy. Organizations take comfort in stability and find that this brings more consistent results.

team-oriented culture: Team-oriented organizational cultures are characterized as placing an emphasis on employee collaboration and cooperation. Employees often play a role in evaluating colleagues. There is a sense among employees across all levels of the hierarchy that positive relationship with each other is vital for a successful workplace.

values: A set of principles or standards that guides a person's behaviors. Values are judgments of what is important to a person, and they influence how one lives and works.

CREDIT

IMG 5.1: Copyright © 2016 Unsplash/Tim Gouw.

CHAPTER 6

Advice You Can Use From Faculty

One group of people who will be influential during your college years are the faculty. Your faculty will help guide and instruct you. I have been in higher education for over 25 years, and in those years, I have had many frank conversations with my colleagues about guiding students. One thing that is evident is faculty care deeply about students and their future success. If you take only one thing away from reading this book, know that your faculty truly want you to see them as a resource. Resources work best when they are used. I have asked faculty across the national to share their advice for undergraduate students. This chapter has grouped the advice into categories or themes. Each category of advice is discussed, and each section ends with an actionable prompt to help you use the advice given. As you read the chapter, make notes on the pages about how the advice and suggestions translate to you and your university.

Knowing Available Resources and Using Them

As of 2017, there are 4,313 institutions of higher education in the United States (Statista, 2017). Every college and university takes pride in having established resources for students to use. The most common student resources available at many colleges and universities include academic advising, a bursar's office or financial services, the career center, dining, disability resources and services centers, a scholarships support office, a health center, residential living, international student services, a counseling center, legal services, library services, a diversity and inclusion office, a Title IV officer, parent and family programing, an alumni office, a recreation

IMG 6.1

center, a student life center, technology services, a study abroad office, transportation services or shuttles, college food banks, childcare, a writing center, a speech lab, and tutoring. Most resources are prepaid and part of your tuition and fees. The Center for First-Generation Student Success (nd) reports that only 16–17% of students do not utilize the career services on their campuses. More students, 30–36%, use the academic support services on their campus (Center for First-Generation Student Success, n.d.).

Some students are the very first in their family to attend college. First-generation students may not have the same advantages as non-first-generation students in having family members who are familiar with the university system. First-generation students represent 50% of students in the United States (Jacimovic, 2021). Many colleges and universities have dedicated programs to serve first-generation students. For example, San Antonio's Trinity University developed the Allies First-Generation, Underrepresented Students Program (Trinity University, n.d.); the state of Texas has an initiative called Generation Texas (GenTX, 2021) focused on increasing the graduation rates of students especially for first-generation students; and Colorado State University offers a First Generation Award. If you are a first-generation student,

---

SPOTLIGHT ON COMMUNICATION
The Learning Organization Theory

The focus of learning organization theory is the way an organization and its members learn and adapt using various resources. Some of the early researchers to write about learning organization theory were Senge et al. (1999). Examining how organizations evolve and continue to adapt to the environment is an important consideration. Senge et al. argue that a learning organization is a group of people who are continually enhancing their capabilities to reach a goal. You can adopt this sentiment for your own personal education and how you approach learning from your faculty. Your faculty are a wealth of information and advice; using their guidance is a key component to college. Senge et al. assert that members of an organization may lack the tools and resources and rely on the organization to provide resources and learning structures. Embracing the principles of learning organization theory, you need to use the structure of higher education to your advantage, so you evolve and productively move toward your post-graduation goals.

feel empowered to seek out the resources to support your work in college. This first advice from a faculty member is directed at first-generation students.

Dr. Cory Young

Position: Associate professor of communication management and design
Institution: Ithaca College, NY

Dr. Cory Young (2019) encourages first generation college students to use the available resources, including those financial, emotional, psychological, and academic. According to the Center for First-Generation Student Success (nd), less first-generation students meet with academic advisors (55%) than non-first-generation students (72%). Also, 14% of first-generation students used student health services, whereas 29% of non-first-generations students did so. As for financial aid services, 65% of first-generation students and 49% non-first-generation students used the services. It is important to become aware of what resources and services your university offers to support you. Never be shy about using the services available. Remember the university invested in the resource to serve the students who need it. If you use service or resources, you are not alone.

Young also reminds you that you got into college for a reason. Hold on to this and enjoy the journey.

Dr. Leslie Ramos Salazar

Position: Associate professor of business communication and decision management
Institution: West Texas A&M University

It is very common for universities to have a student success center. Housed in these centers are services and people dedicated to helping students reach their full potential. Success coaches are advisors you can meet with and share your experiences, both in and out of the classroom. Success centers usually offer workshops and individual sessions on effective note taking, test taking, time management, and staying motivated. Salazar reminds you to utilize the writing and speech center to help you improve and refine your written and oral assignments prior to submitting them to your faculty.

In addition to student success centers, Salazar calls your attention to visiting your university's career service center. In this office you will find assistance with resume and cover letter writing. You can receive help preparing for interviews and even practice interviewing skills in a mock interview. Career services staff are networked with many employers. Part of their job is creating relationship with employers who are looking to hire graduates. Get to know the staff and what organizations they have connected with. Share with them your dream job and organizations. See if they can assist you in the short term as well as the long term to pursue your dream. Keep an eye on when and where career fairs and expos are, and attend as frequently as you can. As you introduce yourself to fair and expo attendees, you will have a chance to practice networking skills. Even as a first- and second-year student, you will find the attendees will be impressed by your initiative and often will provide you with their business card and an invitation to follow up closer to graduation. Also, while at the career fair and expo, you will have a chance to observe other students and pick up tips on how to dress, network, and behave.

> ### EXERCISE 6.1
> ### Prompts for Finding Resources
>
> 1. Spend an afternoon looking up the resources and services your university offers. Make notes on ones you would be interested in learning more about. Be sure to follow up.
> 2. If you haven't already, draft a resume and have a career service staff review it and offer suggestions for improvement.

Connecting With Faculty and Staff

Mr. Peter Marian

Position: Instructor of management
Institution: Saint Leo University, FL

Building a working relationship with faculty or an academic advisor is important. While in college your advisor will not only help you create course schedules each semester but also provide coaching regarding careers and graduate schools. Marian advises you to stay in touch with faculty and advisors after graduation. Faculty and advisors often have the pulse of the industry, and as you continue to grow your career faculty may be of help connecting you with new opportunities. Marian feels students need to create a LinkedIn account and update it on successes often. It is important to start this early in your college career, as it helps get you on the radar of others. Have a goal regarding how you use LinkedIn. You may find that LinkedIn is a great tool for working on the SWOT analysis completed in Chapter 4.

Dr. Cory Young

Position: Associate professor of communication management and design
Institution: Ithaca College, NY

Young advises first-year students to develop good relationships with faculty from the very beginning. To do this, attend office hours at least once a month. To put this in perspective, this is only three times a semester. During office hours, you may want to discuss expectations for an assignment or get clarification on what you did wrong on an exam or assignment. The goal of your visits is to engage in dialogue to develop your relationship with the faculty. It is helpful to have a list of some topics appropriate to discuss during office hours. Talk about the current class you are taking with the faculty as well as a future class the faculty teaches.

> **EXERCISE 6.2**
> **Prompts for Connecting With Faculty and Staff**
>
> 1. Visit faculty office hours for the classes you are currently taking at least three times per semester.
> 2. Visit a few of the faculty you had last semester at least one time per semester.

Dr. Leslie Ramos Salazar

Position: Associate professor of business communication and decision management
Institution: West Texas A&M University

Salazar reiterates the importance of connecting with professors early as a way for laying the foundation for future letters of recommendation you will need in your senior year. The more professors know about you, the stronger the letters will be. Also, they will think of you when they learn about internship and job opportunities. Salazar also suggests that during class you offer input and stay engaged in the class. This is a means of helping faculty remember you. All students leave an impression on faculty; be sure the impression you leave is one of a professional and diligent worker.

Making the Most of Teamwork and Communication

Demonstrating effective teamwork and communication are always top of the list of desired skills for new employees. The key is understanding how to capture both on a resume, in a cover letter, and during a job interview. Faculty have advice about being an effective team member and competent communicator.

Dr. Ioannis Pantzalis

Position: Associate professor of marketing
Institution: Saint Leo University, FL

Teamwork and communication are key in class group projects. It would be rare to not encounter group work during your time in college. Faculty embed group work because employers share that it is an important skill for employees to possess. College is a great time to practice your skill in being a team leader and a follower. Pantzalis shares that group projects involve time management, motivating uncooperative members, and avoiding groupthink. Experience in all three will result in great examples that could be shared in a future interview. Keep notes as you work on projects regarding the trials your group faced and how they were resolved. It is common for the employment interview to include questions about how you dealt with difficult conversations or working with difficult people.

Dr. Pallavi Eswara

Position: Director of the Office of Postdoctoral Affairs
Institution: Pennsylvania State University

In a 2019 article in *Inside Higher Ed*, Eswara (2019) offers advice for students on improving their teamwork skills. Although the article was focused on graduate students, the advice applies to undergraduate students. The key skills you will need to master and be able to demonstrate through your experiences include good communication, emotional intelligence, motivational abilities, and relationship management. To be a good (competent) communicator you will need to explain ideas clearly, use active listening skills, understand nonverbal communication, and establish how to prevent and manage conflicts. Emotional intelligence (EQ) is a trendy concept in business. In short, EQ refers the skill of recognizing your own emotions as well as others' and using emotional information to guide your thinking and behavior. Having a high EQ demonstrates you have the ability to show empathy and trust within your group. Motivational abilities include motivating others, being a positive influence on others, asking appropriate and good questions, identifying team goals, and increasing engagement of members. The last opportunity Eswara says group work can provide is showcasing relationship management skills. These skills include showing respect for others and their ideas and work as well as taking responsibility for your work and role in the group.

Pallavi Eswara, "Developing Your Teamwork Skills," *Inside Higher Ed*. Copyright © 2019 by Inside Higher Ed.

EXERCISE 6.3
Prompts for Demonstrating Teamwork and Communication

1. Test your EQ by taking a free quiz at https://www.ihhp.com/free-eq-quiz/.

2. Keep notes about group projects, so you can refer to your experience when you are preparing for interviews.

Creating Your Personal Brand

Dr. Ioannis Pantzalis

Position: Associate professor of marketing
Institution: Saint Leo University, FL

In Chapter 3, you read about the importance of creating a personal brand. Your personal brand represents who you are as a professional. Pantzalis emphasizes the value of creating your personal brand and offers suggestions for how to go about it. He suggests you create a website for your professional brand management. Include things such as blogs, videos, podcasts, pictures, portfolio pieces, and accomplishments. Not only can a website serve as your portfolio, but it can demonstrate your understanding of creating a following and interest. Most website hosting companies offer basic analytics for understanding the traffic on your website. Explore using and understanding the analytics. Speaking about social media analytics will help set you apart from other applicants. Pantzalis asserts there are topics you should understand as you head into your career. These topics include focus, grit, memory improvement, gamification of individual goals, and accelerated acquisition of new skills. Specifically, with focus, Pantzalis advises you to examine how you waste time and identify the key activities and focus your energy on them. Grit refers how to stick to the task no matter how challenging. Grit reflects your determination and motivation for pursuing long-term

---

EXERCISE 6.4
Prompts for Establishing a Personal Brand

1. Define what your personal brand is or what you want it to be. How are you going to showcase it to a prospective employer?
2. Explore and learn one tactic each semester on how to quickly learn new skills.

---

goals, even when failure, challenges, or adversity occurs. Your passion and perseverance for your goals determine your grit. It is important to have a good memory. Often, intern supervisors comment that interns don't remember the details of the instructions given for tasks and need to ask for instructions to be repeated. Explore different tactics for improving your memory. Gamification is popular with marketers to get consumers to engage with the products. McDonald's, for example, often offers a way for customers to play a game of Monopoly. Consumers collect properties on the game board in hopes of winning free food or money. Have you played? If so, then you participated in a gamified marketing campaign. Pantzalis suggests that you find ways to gamify your goals. You will find that you are more likely to reach your goals. Much of what is discussed in this book is identifying skills and acquiring new ones. Pantzalis suggests developing tactics for accelerated acquisition of new skills. This includes determining the best techniques to concentrate.

> **EXERCISE 6.5**
> **Prompts for Investing in Others**
>
> 1. Come up with three ways you can invest time in people.
> 2. Determine a feasible way you could volunteer your time helping others. Try to connect it to a skill(s) you are gaining in your major—for example, teaching the elderly how to use email, social media, or a smartphone to communicate with family members.

Investing in Others

Dr. Ismael Lopez Medel

Position: Associate professor and coordinator of public relations
Institution: Azusa Pacific University, CA

Medel reminds you to invest in other people. Be impactful. Whether it is helping classmates or volunteering when faculty are asking for student representatives, show up for others. As other faculty have advised, build solid relationships with others. Not only will it make you feel good, but it provides opportunities for you to practice your communication and relational skills. Find ways to invest in others. For example, if your major does not have a mentoring program, suggest starting one. With the help of others seek out local business people to serve as mentors to students. Or suggest partnering students in a senior capstone class with students in a first-year introductory class. Investing time in others allows for connections to be created and a chance to understand others' stories. Medel also recommends that as you invest in others, use these experiences to step outside your comfort zone to grow.

International Experiences

Dr. Ismael Lopez Medel

Position: Associate professor and coordinator of public relations
Institution: Azusa Pacific University, CA

Medel advises you to think internationally. International experiences help you not only make memories, but they also help you grow as a person. You have learned throughout your communication major that perspective is a key concept in the process of communication. Studying abroad is a great experience that will help demonstrate many different skills and characteristics a future employer will find desirable. Consider studying abroad or interning for a semester in another country. Many countries offer study aboard program for communication majors. Be sure to work with your university's study abroad office to ensure credits transfer to your major.

> **EXERCISE 6.6**
> **Prompts for Having International Experiences**
>
> 1. Research your university's study abroad options for your major. Are there any you are interested in?
> 2. Examine the tuition fees associated with study abroad. Often, the difference is the cost of a plane ticket.

Dr. Mary Dwyer & Ms. Courtney K. Peters

Position: President of IES Abroad; Communications and media relations coordinator
Institution: TransitionsAbroad.com

Dwyer and Peters (2021) offer a great list of benefits of studying abroad during college. There are many benefits of studying abroad, including personal growth and taking time to learn about yourself away from what you are most familiar with. This would demonstrate grit and other attributes Pantzalis recommended. Studying abroad provides you the chance to explore a culture you have longed to experience or a new destination you've wanted to visit. The program, A Semester at Sea, offers a unique study abroad program that includes living on a cruise ship and visiting over 20 ports of call around the world. All study abroad programs offer an opportunity enriched with meeting new people and forming friendships. Host families often become treasured family members. Traveling provides an opportunity to change your worldview. There is a large world out there with diverse people. Your travels and experience studying abroad could be the first step to being a future global leader by gaining an understanding of culture, politics, and economic systems. Intercultural competence can be nurtured and strengthened with an immersion experience in another country. If your future career has a global component, it would be valuable for you to consider studying abroad. Experience living abroad provides a chance for you to acquire new skills for your intended career path. One valuable skill would be a foreign language.

Mary M. Dwyer and Courtney K. Peters, "The Benefits of Study Abroad," *IES Abroad*. Copyright © 2004 by IES Abroad.

Job Interview Preparation and Expectations

Dr. Ioannis Pantzalis

Position: Associate professor of marketing
Institution: Saint Leo University, FL

Pantzalis reminds you to start preparing for job interviews early. Even early in your college experience you can practice interviewing skills. Understand the difference between generic things you should do for every interview and customized things you should do for the specific job you are interviewing for. Use the career services office to learn about the difference. Find opportunities to network through events, online, alumni, faculty, and staff. Don't save these tasks for your senior year.

Strategically Use Internships

Mr. Peter Marian

Position: Instructor of management
Institution: Saint Leo University, FL

Approach internships in three different ways: Use an internship (1) as a "foot in the door" to land a job right after graduation; (2) as a test to see if this is the industry or job you really want to pursue; and (3) to add more experience to your resume.

Dr. Candace A. Roberts

Position: Professor of education and director, Center for Teaching and Learning Excellence
Institution: Saint Leo University, FL

According to Roberts, internships are like arranged marriages. You don't get to pick your partner, but you have to live with them. Ingredients of a successful marriage and internship include the following: don't judge (and if you do, keep it to yourself); be patient; be humble; work as hard as you've ever worked; keep communication positive and open; and ask for feedback. Remember that people (even supervisors or leaders) are flawed—forgive, and let it go. Unlike marriages, internships are short; you can do anything for a semester or year. Time is on your side. Keep your eye on your goal: experience and a positive recommendation.

Get Involved

> **EXERCISE 6.7**
> **Prompts for Thinking About Internships**
>
> 1. Look for internships, and group them according to the three different approaches Marian suggested. Which internships are great for getting your foot in the door? Which are great for testing out the industry or job? And which would be great on a resume.
>
> 2. Identify your wish list for what you would hope an internship site supervisor would write about in a letter of recommendation. Be mindful of what you will need to do to make this a reality.

Dr. Leslie Ramos Salazar

Position: Associate professor of business communication and decision management
Institution: West Texas A&M University

The wonderful thing about college life is that it is a bustling hub of activity. Getting involved helps you own your experience and feel connected to the college. First-year students need to aim to connect with student organizations. If there is no specific one you are interested in, consider starting one. Universities can be large and isolating, especially if you are not connected to people. Go to different club meetings, and try out the ones you are most interested in. The more you are involved, the more connected and invested you will be in your education. Be mindful not to over extend yourself. For commuter students, it is key to be involved with campus activities, as it is easy to feel disconnected with the university, faculty, and peers.

Skills Expectations

Dr. Scott Britten

> **EXERCISE 6.8**
> **Prompts for Getting Involved**
>
> 1. Research different student organizations offered on your campus. Make a list of potential organizations to join based on your major and interests.
> 2. Pair up with a peer from one of your communication classes, and be a "club buddy," helping each other stay motivated to attend meetings and events.

Position: Associate dean, liberal arts & sciences
Institution: Milwaukee Area Technical College, WI

As a communication major you will be expected to have certain skills by future employers. Among the most sought after skills are top-notch writing and oral skills, along with cultural awareness and interpersonal skills. To land your first job, you will need to develop and be prepared to showcase a particular skill set. For example, you might need to know message campaign design, coding, database management, personnel management, media production, or something else you can present, preferably via portfolio, to a potential employer. There are other skills known as soft skills or power skills that are considered to be transferable from one job to another. Some of the power skills include teamwork, leadership, empathy, problem-solving, critical thinking, adaptability, initiative, and entrepreneurialism. Hard skills are those that are connected to specific knowledge, training, and experience. Revisit chapter 2 for more on the different types of skills.

> **EXERCISE 6.9**
> **Prompts for Collecting Skills**
>
> 1. Revisit chapter 2 and your inventories of your skills. Determine what soft skills as well as hard skills you possess. What can you improve upon?
> 2. At the start of each semester, review your syllabi, and take note of what soft and hard skills you will be learning or practicing.

> **TOOLS FOR ADVICE YOU CAN USE FROM FACULTY**
>
> Here is a list of resources to watch and read. Each reinforces the topics presented in the chapter.
>
> **Michelle Miller-Adams (2020): "Professor Offers Best Advice for College Freshmen"**
>
> **READ AT** https://grownandflown.com/professors-advice-for-college/
>
>
>
> **Deborah J. Cohan (2018): "College Professor Advice: 16 Things You Should Never Do As a Student"**
>
> **READ AT** https://www.teenvogue.com/story/16-things-you-should-never-say-college-professors
>
>
>
> **Dustin Wax (2017): "Advice for Students: How to Talk to Professors"**
>
> **READ AT** https://www.lifehack.org/articles/communication/advice-for-students-how-to-talk-to-professors.html
>
>

CREDITS

IMG 6.1: Copyright © 2019 Unsplash/Dollar Gill.
IMG 6.2: Copyright © 2019 Unsplash/Felicia Buitenwerf.

CHAPTER 7

Finding Your Seat on the Bus

To be a successful job candidate you need to understand how great companies operate, develop a vision, and determine how they will use their employees to collectively carry out their vision and mission. There is no better way to prepare to enter an industry than learning an organization's strategy for success. Human capital is the skills, knowledge, and experience of employees who are viewed as valuable by an organization. Jim Collins is a noteworthy author, who has written several books about what makes companies more than just successful—what makes them great. One of his most popular books, *Good to Great*, was published in 2001 and is still seen as relevant. Collins coaches executive leaders how to build a great company. I recommend you read this book. You might think it is not something that interests you, or you might be wondering what a book on business strategy has to do with you and your success in college and the workforce. I strongly believe reading this book will have a great impact on your success upon graduation. Why? Robert Baden-Powell said, "If you make yourself indispensable to your employer, [they are] not going to part with you in a hurry no matter what it costs [them]" (The HR Gurus, 2018). Consider this advice the key to being a successful employee, no matter the career or industry. Most companies will employ cross-training to ensure they are not dependent on a single employee. For you, the employee, your goal should be contributing to the organization in such a way that makes you and your work valuable to the company. In this chapter we explore some of the ideas advanced by Collins from the perspective of the employee. Throughout this chapter Collins's ideas will be discussed and applied to you as college student.

Being a Bus Rider

Collins (2001) uses the metaphor of a bus to explain how organizations become great organizations. Many organizations are good companies and turn a profit; however, less are actually great companies. In the metaphor, the bus driver is the organizational leader, and the bus represents the organization. Read the following passage from *Good to Great*:

> You are a bus driver. The bus, your company, is at a standstill, and it's your job to get it going. You have to decide where you're going, how you're going to get there, and who's going with you.
>
> Most people assume that great bus drivers (read: business leaders) immediately start the journey by announcing to the people on the bus where they're going—by setting a new direction or by articulating a fresh corporate vision.
>
> In fact, leaders of companies that go from good to great start not with "where" but with "who." They start by getting the right people on the bus, the wrong people off the bus, and the right people in the right seats. And they stick with that discipline—first the people, then the direction—no matter how dire the circumstances. (Collins, 2001)

What are the lessons from this passage? How does it apply to your college and career journey? Your personal goal is to be the right person for the organization you desire to work for. With a college degree in hand, the goal should not be to get any job. Rather, you should strive to find the best organization for you—one that aligns with your values and skills. We spoke earlier about how understanding an organization's mission statement and how you can contribute to delivering it on behalf of the company is important. Every aspect of this passage applies to you as a college student. First, you could apply this passage to your decision of major. Be committed to your major. If it is not the right fit, change it. There are often different kinds of students, when it comes to choosing a major. One group is steadfast on a specific idea of a major or career. Even when they struggle in classes or are miserable, they don't quickly change majors. Others adapt to change and explore different majors, until they find the best fit. Embrace exploration. Make sure you are on the right bus. While in college, faculty can be seen as your bus drivers. Be aware of the objectives of each class you take. The class too could be viewed as a bus. It is important you apply strategy to your approach to being a student in each of your classes. I think you can consider yourself the business driver too! Your career could be seen as your bus. It is important to surround yourself with the right people for your journey. The ultimate lesson from Collins's bus metaphor is that your career journey is dynamic, and you will count on others you encounter along your journey to help shape your career.

One of Collins's (2001) concepts is **disciplined people**. For Collins this refers to who is on the bus. As you read in the previous passage, having the right people on the bus and in the right seats is vital to success. It is important to find the right bus and people that are aligned with your destination, goals, and personal ethics. This is huge. Reread those words. As a college student you may often feel you are not in control of your destiny because you are taking prescribed courses for a specific major. Very few colleges have majors in which students have complete freedom over what courses they take for their degree. There is a reason for this. Programs must meet regional accreditation requirements. Faculty use courses to meet assessment goals for the major. You take classes in a specific sequence and complete specific assignments for a reason. My advice is to apply the principles from Collins and make sure the bus (major) you are on meets the vision you have for your goal. Feel empowered to ask your advisor or department chair to make course substitutions, so you are able to take certain classes that best align with your vision. How do you do this? First, become very familiar with the course offerings of not just your department and major but across the university. You might be surprised how many business, psychology, and political science classes fit nicely with communication. Highlight the courses you are most excited to take and that match your goals. Next, arrange a meeting with your advisor, and discuss your goals and classes that will help you reach your goals. Ask for help figuring out how they could be included in your program of courses. You might be surprised of the outcome. As a communication student, I was most interested in the student of conflict. I was able to take classes in aggression and violence in criminal justice to help deepen my understanding of related concepts. I recall my faculty being very helpful and supportive. Your advisor might even see an opportunity for a minor that supports your interests and adds value to your major—and ultimately your career goals.

Collins (2001) warns about being aware of a shift in destinations. If you find that your courses or major no longer aligns with your goals, ask yourself why. It is common for students to change majors, sometimes often. This is because this is a critical time in your life. You are growing and changing as you explore new areas of life as a college student. If you realize you are less connected to your classes and faculty, it could be a signal that you are on the wrong bus. I recall in an organizational communication class, students completed an assignment called Me, Myself and a Career in Organizational Communication. This assignment required self-assessments to determine student's values, passions, and skills. They did a SWOT analysis, just as you did earlier in this book. I required students to present their finding to the class, and one semester a student realized she was in the wrong major. I am passionate about communication, and it would never be my intention to sway your away from the communication major. But as you learn more about the field, you change. It happens. Never be afraid to recognize that you might be in the wrong major. Faculty want to see students succeed. Faculty want to see students engaged in their major and courses. There is no better way to be engaged than to be passionate about the subject. I would also suggest exploring the internet to see how other university package majors and minors. Often, you might see something you could advocate for at your own university.

Years ago I was teaching in a department that required communication majors to complete a senior project. The project was similar to a thesis. Prior to taking the senior project course, students had to successfully complete a communication theory course. Many students realized what I already know; they were missing a research methods class. Over the course of two years or so, students in the student project class would advocate for the development of a research methods class. They knew such a class would make the senior project class easier. Students saw that they were lacking the proper tools to complete the project. It was not long after that I was able to develop that very class. My advice is to be an active participant in your major. Talk to your fellow students to see what they would like to see added to the course offerings. Talk with advisors and faculty.

Don't forget minors and double majors are great options. It can be said that minors do not get student jobs, but they do provide more substance for your professional narrative. Select minors for how they can contribute support for different aspects of your story. For example, you might select a minor in Spanish because you know that being an international correspondent requires fluency in a second language. You may decide to minor in art history, which may not seemingly be related to communication; however, what if you decide to earn this minor through a study abroad experience? If you are interested in multimedia aspects of communication you might be interested in having a computer science minor. Imagine how competitive a video or social media creator would be in the job market if they also had HTML knowledge? Another minor you might consider is something in business. A trend I have seen at my own university is communication majors taking on a double major or minor in accounting or economics. Do you know it is common for investment banking teams assigned to a client to include relational managers? Banking is not all about the numbers. Financial companies look to hire communication majors because of their ability to create effective messages and relate with others. Communication is everywhere. Communication can be found in every industry. Did you start out as a premed student? Maybe you switched your major to communication. Did you know that every hospital employs communication professionals? Many private medical practices are using social media directors to enhance the marketing of their practice.

Getting on the Right Bus

It is important to identify the qualities of the right seat on the right bus for you and evaluate every potential job by these criteria. Consider the organization's culture, and determine what type of organization you are best suited for. Examine the values and mission of the organization. Do they align with yours? Consider the level of communication present in the organization and the specific department your position is located in. Is there a sense of transparency? Do you require a high degree of transparency? Consider the teambuilding present in the organization and the department. Does it match your expectations? Does the organization invest in people? What does this look like, and does it align with your goals? When you are interviewing, consider the process. How long does it take the hiring manager to reply to your emails? Reflect on how the organization pitches themselves to you. Or is the focus of the conversation just on what you will do for them? Collin's metaphor of the bus emphasizes that you need to locate the right organization that has plenty of seats (positions) for growth in your career. Great companies to work for are those that invest in people and look for ways to grow them and their careers—not just for the betterment of the organization but the person. Determine in your own mind by reviewing different artifacts how much the organization will value you as an employee.

Once you are in the job consider how often you are bored and whether you are being listened to. Do you feel drained by the job? These may be signs you are on the wrong bus. You will be invested in the overall success of the organization in getting the bus where it is mean to go. This requires you to be a team player, and your participation is imperative to the success of the organization and your own success. It is easier to be a team player when you feel included and see a future for yourself on the bus. Everyone on the bus needs to be self-motivated. We know the bus will not go, or at least not go in the intended direction, unless the efforts of all employees collectively endorse the direction of the bus (the mission of the organization). Everyone, including you, on the bus needs to be united in their effort to get the bus where it's supposed to go.

With all this talk about "the bus" and its "destination," it would be easy to misinterpret Collins's message. The focus should be whether the organization's destination aligns with your values, ethics, and career goals. The organization's goals and objectives might change; therefore, it is important for you to genuinely like and believe in the success of the employees you work with. Have you ever taken a long bus ride? It is always more enjoyable (and time passes more quickly) when you enjoy the company of your fellow travelers. You spend less time asking, "Are we there yet?" Be aware of the changes in the destination. You may find that this bus is not right for you anymore because its goals are no longer aligned with your goals and ethics. This is the one reason people leave jobs. Suddenly, they want to be on another bus heading someplace new. As you learn more about the communication industry, consider which organizations and positions might be a fit for you as you start your career and which ones will be later stops on your career journey.

EXERCISE 7.1
What Organizational Position Are You Best Suited For?

Use the following table to record some of the organizations and positions that might be a fit for you after you graduate and the ones that might be a fit later in your career journey. After you complete the table, consider discussing it with an advisor, faculty member, mentor, or career services staff member. Look for insights from more experienced individuals. Keep notes on what feedback you received. Look for suggestions of similar organizations.

Time in Career	First Job in Field	Second Job in Field	Mid-career Job in Field	Aspirational Job in Field
Organization				
Position				
Why?				
Feedback From Others/Similar Organizations to Consider				

You will notice that the last window of the bus in Exercise 7.2 is how you know it is time to move on. What we know about organizational success is that you must have the right people on the bus, in the right seats, performing the right tasks. If any of these things are wrong, success is challenging. From an individual's perspective you will learn to recognize if the wrong people are on the bus. If so, how does it impact how you perform your job? It is important to know if you are on the wrong bus, not only for the organization's benefit but for your own success and happiness as well. It was mentioned earlier that one reason people leave jobs is for career growth, and another is because of bosses. Often, you will recognize that the organization's morals are no longer aligned with yours through your experience working with your boss. You might also note if the job you are performing is not

> **EXERCISE 7.2**
> **Describing Your Bus**
>
>
>
> A helpful exercise describing your bus—the type of organizations you are drawn to and see as being a good fit.
>
> | On the Bus … | Questions to Ask | Answers |
> |---|---|---|
> | Window 1 is the driver | What are the characteristics of the type of boss you work best with? What are some you cannot work with? | |
> | Window 2 is the organization | What would you need to be part of the organization's mission statement? | |
> | Window 3 is the coworkers | What do you need from coworkers to be your best at work? | |
> | Window 4 is the potential for the group | How would need to be invested in by leadership to feel appreciated and valued? | |
> | Window 5 is your nonnegotiables | How will you know it is time to leave the organization? | |

what was advertised. You might be on the wrong seat on the bus. This happens when you are happy with the organization and its direction, but you are overqualified or underqualified for a specific job. Some organizations recognize internal talent and are willing to move employees around. This is commonly achieved with internal restructuring. One last piece of sage advice is to listen to yourself. You might be on the wrong bus or the wrong seat if your coworkers do not value you or listen to your opinions. Also, if you are complaining a great deal to others, it is sign the bus or seat needs to be changed. You may have experienced this in your college major. If you changed majors, you experienced changing seats on the bus. If you have transferred and changed universities, you have experienced getting off one bus and getting on another bus.

SPOTLIGHT ON COMMUNICATION
Organizational Systems Theory

There are many different aspects of organizational communication theory that can be connected to Jim Collins's ideas. One that will be discussed here is **organizational systems theory**. Systems theory was first applied to the study of organizations by Katz and Khan (1966). One of the core assumptions is that the whole is greater than the sum of its parts. In other words, organizations are based on people, and this effort is not understood as a simple addition problem. Systems theory is an approach to studying organization as a set of interdependent parts, each with its own specific function and interrelated responsibilities. The magic of organizations is what happens among the people. One of my favorite analogies to use for this concept is baking brownies. When you bake brownies you gather each ingredient, you mix them together, and then you place them in the oven to bake. When the brownies are done and served, no person ever says, "Great eggs" or "Great milk." Instead they say, "Great brownies." The individual ingredients are important, but what is more important is the magic that happens in the oven. According to Collins, this is the hope of every organization. If you have the right ingredients, the organization can rise to greatness. As an employee you should be focused on finding the organization that best fits you, so you, as an ingredient, can participate in the magic of organizational activity to, hopefully, produce greatness—or brownies.

There are other assumptions of system theory that are helpful to understanding how the theory can be applied to you and your career journey. The first assumption, as we discussed, is that a system must be understood as a whole and not its parts. Another assumption is that systems are self-reflexive, meaning they are characterized by their ability to make themselves and their own behavior the focus of examination. You are a system and have the power and ability to reflect on your behaviors, make adjustments, and set new goals. Also, you are able to look at what influences your behaviors, decisions, and such. You do not have to be passive toward the influences; rather, you can make adjustments. One of my favorite assumptions of the system theory is the concept of "equifinality." **Equifinality** posits there are many different routes one can take to achieve a goal. Consider two groups of people being tasked with folding a fitted bed sheet. No other directions were provided—just fold the sheet into a neat square. One group might start by folding the corners to create a crisp edge. The other might start by folding the sheet lengthwise. Regardless of the specific steps each group used, the result is a folded fitted sheet. Another example is going home at the holidays. You may choose to drive, fly, take a train, or take a bus. At the end of your journey you arrive home. The goal is reaching your destination, regardless of the method of transportation. This is an excellent principle to keep in mind as you begin your career journey. No two careers journeys are carbon copies. Embrace the many routes that can lead you to an enriching and rewarding career.

Other concepts of system theory that are helpful include hierarchy, feedback, and boundaries. **Hierarchy** refers to the layers each system has, which suggests systems

(continued ...)

are complex. As you work your way through your degree program, you will encounter many of the different layers. In some ways, this is related to networking. Recognize the many layers of the college experience. Every system has a **feedback** loop. As a college student, you are fortunate to have the ability to gain feedback from several different sources. Your faculty, peers, and internship supervisors will all provide feedback. Invest time in developing skills to receive and use helpful feedback. The final concept I will discuss are the **boundaries** that make the system. Each system lives in a supra system. You live within your university, and your university lives in a state, region, country, and the like. You also have subsystems that live within your university. There are majors, departments, living communities, student clubs, honor societies, sororities and fraternities, and many more. Boundaries define membership in a system. You might wear your university's logo on your hoodie. Some boundaries are flexible, and others are rigid. Flexible boundaries allow for flow in and out. Rigidity regulates the flow in and out, making it harder to get in. It is helpful to reflect on the different subsystems you are involved in and how to make use of them as you work toward your goals.

Organizational system theory is a helpful framework for viewing your academic life. Using some of the concepts can provide you with tools to use as you navigate your major and your career. It is important to see that all the experiences you encounter while in college are the parts that will make up the whole. One event is most likely not going to define you; rather, over the years, your cumulative experience will help create the professional you become.

TOOLS FOR FINDING YOUR SEAT ON THE BUS

Here is a list of resources to watch and read. Each reinforces the topics presented in the chapter.

Lisa Whealon (2017):" Finding The 'Right Seat On The Bus'"

WATCH AT https://www.forbes.com/sites/forbeshumanresourcescouncil/2017/04/04/finding-the-right-seat-on-the-bus/?sh=7a3702ad62ad

(continued ...)

Kinesis, Inc. (2015): "Leaders of Great Companies Ask: First Who, Then What?"

WATCH AT https://www.kinesisinc.com/first-who-then-what/

Dave Kraft (2020): "10 Ways to Know If You're in the Wrong Seat on the Bus"

WATCH AT https://davekraft.org/2020/02/11/10-ways-to-know-if-youre-on-the-wrong-seat-in-the-bus/

KEY TERMS

boundaries: The system theory of organizations refer to boundaries to define membership in a system.

disciplined people: Author Jim Collins term that refers to who's on the bus or in the organization. Having the right people on the bus and in the right seats is vital to success. In this book you are encouraged to consider the bus as your major and intended career.

equifinality: Equifinality is part of the system theory or organizations and refers to the different ways of getting to the same result.

feedback: Feedback is part of the communication process. It requires communicators to provide verbal or nonverbal response to another's message.

hierarchy: From the organizational systems theory, hierarchy refers to the layers each system has, which suggests systems are complex.

organizational systems theory: Systems theory is an approach to studying organization as a set of interdependent parts, each with its own specific function and interrelated responsibilities.

CREDIT

IMG 7.1: Copyright © 2015 Unsplash/Matthew Henry.

CHAPTER 8

Industry Advice

You know how much experience and education your faculty have and that they serve as great role models and mentors. Voices from industry professionals are also great sources of information. Throughout the book it has been emphasized that you need to become savvy in developing a professional network. Recommendations on working with the professionals have been woven throughout the chapters. The purpose of this chapter is to extend what has already been shared and discuss a few leaders from industry. As you read through the advice offered by professionals, ask yourself how you can best make use of it.

> **SPOTLIGHT ON COMMUNICATION**
> **Constructivism**
>
> Constructivism is theory that explains individual differences in the ability to communicate skillfully in social situations. The fundamental premise of constructivism is that we make sense of the world through a collection of constructs. In this sense, constructs are a thought structure we use to make sense of and organize our perceptions. As we go about our day we take in many messages. We have a need for order. We look for patterns and attach meaning to the patterns. As humans, we need our communication structures to have order. We construct meaning of symbols used to communicate by working with others.
>
> As you read this chapter consisting of advice from communication professionals, you will be comparing what you read with what you already know. If there is alignment, you will recognize a pattern, and further meaning will be created. I find it invaluable to bring guest speakers into my classroom. I know that something the professional will tell
>
> (continued ...)

> my students will align with something I said in class. I know that, suddenly, my words will have new meaning because students heard them from a guest speaker. If you find throughout the book I have echoed something your faculty have said to you, recognize it as a pattern and reflection of reality. Use our words to inform your behavior and decisions. As you read this chapter, hopefully some of the advice will be new. Take in the new information, and seek ways to expand on it. If worthy, create a new pattern by looking for others that repeat the same information.
>
> The spirit of this chapter is to encourage you to seek out reality and become an active participate in using this information. At the end of the chapter there are resources for gaining insight in how the COVID-19 pandemic has changed the future of work. You are part of that future. You are walking directly into a world of work that exists in the aftermath of a pandemic. Recognize the power you have to play a vital part in shaping the future of work, creating a new reality.

Mandy Menaker

Company: Shapr
Position: Head of brand

Menaker's advice includes getting better at receiving constructive feedback (Menaker, 2017). As communication majors you are well versed on the communication model and the importance of feedback. Do not overlook the power feedback has on your readiness for the job market. Specifically, Menaker suggests writing down all the feedback you receive and examining it when you have fresh eyes. If appropriate, schedule a follow-up meeting, or visit faculty during office hours to discuss the feedback and ways to improve. For assignments look for themes, and consider how you might improve the weakness observed. For example, your faculty may state you need to support your claims in your writing with clear evidence. This is tremendous feedback that could connect directly to your effectiveness in the job interview. If you have a tendency to be vague and not use examples or sources in your writing, you may do the same in an interview. Keep in mind that prospective employers like to ask questions, looking for attention to detail and support answers. Develop a habit of thanking people for their feedback. You may not do it after each assignment, but at the end of the class, you should find time to follow up with the faculty to thank them for the learning experience and share an example of what you learned or how their feedback (instruction) helped you. This is a great way to build relationships with your faculty.

Mandy Menaker, "10 New Year's Resolutions to Supercharge Your Career," Undercover Recruiter. Copyright © by Undercover Recruiter.

> **EXERCISE 8.1**
> **Prompts for Action**
>
> 1. What is the best method for capturing the feedback you receive? Would creating an Excel file work? Would you rather use a dedicated spiral notebook or journal? The method you select should be indexed or organized in a way allowing you to easily find information when you are ready to revisit it. An Excel file would allow you to add lines as you receive new feedback. This will help you organize feedback according to theme or topic.
>
> 2. Write an example of a "thank you" email you could send to a faculty member who provided helpful feedback. An effective "thank you" note will show appreciation, reference key parts of the conversation, and offer an invitation for future follow-up conversations.

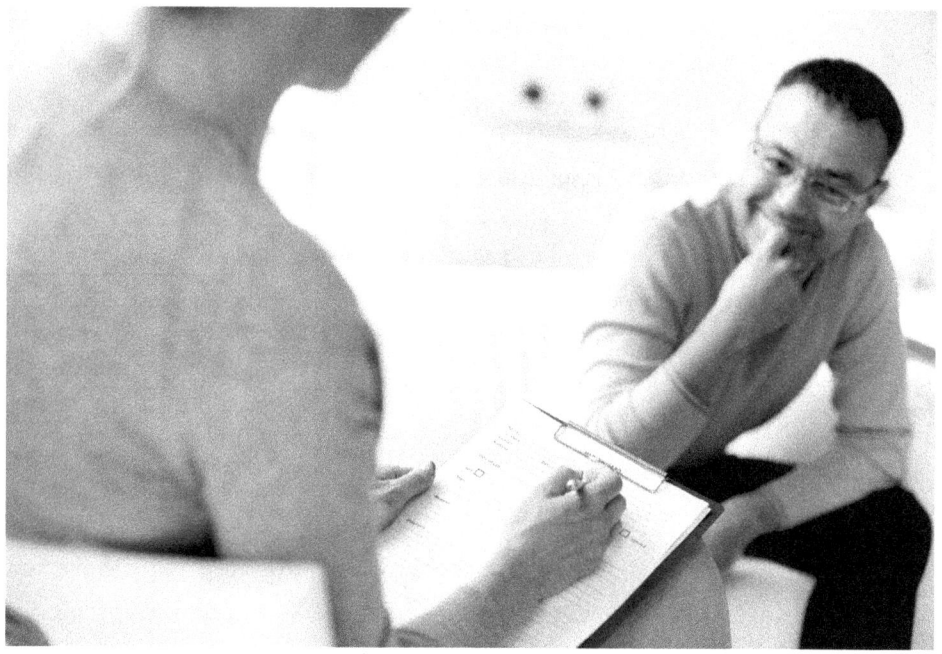

Amanda Ponzar

Company: CHC: Creating Healthier Communities
Position: Chief communications strategy officer

Being able to show results from your work as early as possible is important. By adding statistics to your clips, you're showing employers you are not only a skilled communicator but also that your work is able to return results that prospective employers would want to see on the content you create for them. For your clips themselves,

Ponzar notes that college is a good time to diversify your skillset and add work from many different areas of the communication industry to your portfolio (Forbes, 2019).

Forbes Communications Council, "Considering A Communications Career? 13 Tips For Industry Newcomers," *Forbes*. Copyright © 2019 by Forbes.com LLC.

EXERCISE 8.2
Prompts for Action

1. How does your portfolio represent multichannel pieces? A multichannel piece refers to showcasing more than one skill set, such as writing and using data to make business decisions. What are the skills commonly represented in your portfolio? What are others that could be added? For example, in my intercultural communication class, I require students to do an analysis of diversity, equity, and inclusion statements found on companies' website. What makes my assignment different is that within their brief report, students have to showcase their analysis, formatting (visual communication), and writing skills. The document must include embedded in-text boxes containing some of the DEI statements. Students also have to identify and rewrite weak statements, making them stronger. This assignment showcases more than one skill of students.

2. How skilled are you at social media analytics? How skilled are you at making data-driven decisions?

Stacy Sherman

Company: Schindler Elevator Corp.
Position: Head of customer experience

When you are applying for internships or even preparing to graduate, it is important to remember that you won't get your dream job right away. You cannot go from the bottom to the top overnight, and that's OK. Be patient with yourself, and develop a plan before you take your first internship that will get you where you want to be in a reasonable timeframe. Sherman advises to make sure that plan has some mini goals integrated into it, so you have the chance to celebrate the little wins along the way. Make your connections, and celebrate the success you have now, while you wait for your dream job (Sherman, 2021).

Stacy Sherman, "10 Leadership Strategies To 'Crawl, Walk, Run' Your Way To Success," *Doing CX Right*. Copyright © 2020 by Doing CX Right.

> **EXERCISE 8.3**
> **Prompts for Action**
>
> 1. What are some of your mini goals for your career as a student? What about after?
> 2. How can you become more patient with yourself and progress in college and towards your career? Patience means giving yourself permission to make mistakes, to not know all the answers to questions about your career or future, and to try new things. Develop a list of things you could do to gain more insight into your future career. You may want to make an appointment with your advisor. Your advisor can answer questions and help you create a list of things to do over the semester.

Colby Reade

Company: M. J. Murdock Charitable Trust
Position: Director of communications

College is the perfect time to make connections within your industry. Your university may hold career fairs or other networking events that will help you meet professionals and gather information on the industry you think you would like to be in. Make sure to attend at least one a year if you can, always bring copies of your resume, and dress professionally. You never know who you will meet and how they will impact your career, even if you are just a starting your college career. Reade suggests conducting informational interviews with faculty and industry contacts early on in your college career will help you identify what skills you should be honing while in school and ways you can perfect your portfolio long before you graduate (Forbes, 2019). And again, always dress and comport yourself professionally during these interviews, and be sure to thank the person you are interviewing with for their time.

> **EXERCISE 8.4**
> **Prompts for Action**
>
> 1. Create a plan for connecting with professionals. Start with your career service office on campus. Introduce yourself, and have a conversation with one of the staff members. Let them know what career or careers you are interested in. Ask them they can connect you with people in the field. Perhaps look into opportunities to job shadow. A job shadow is not an internship; rather, it is a short time when you follow around a professional to get a glimpse at the everyday life in a specific career.
> 2. Seek and find the opportunities on campus to network and create connections with others.

Tom Wozniak

Company: OPTIZMO Technologies
Position: Head of marketing

College is the perfect time to try new things! This goes for your career, especially. Even when you've already started your first job in the industry, try different types of marketing and communications positions as well as methods and approaches to diversify your portfolio. While in college, take classes on a wide variety of marketing and communications topics, so you have some practice and clips to add to your portfolio. Wozniak suggests that once you're out of college, don't pigeonhole yourself just yet (Forbes, 2019). There are many different jobs out there in the industry, and knowing a little about a lot of them will help you find the best place for yourself more than just locking yourself in from the beginning without trying anything new.

> **EXERCISE 8.5**
> **Prompts for Action**
>
> 1. Talk with people who work in your desired field, and learn about the different options. Research interviews with or reach out directly to at least three professionals who work in your desired field, and write a paragraph for each about their backgrounds.
> 2. List the top three areas of communication you would like to work in and why. How do these areas differ from each other? What are some interesting roles that fall under each of these areas? How do the daily responsibilities, average salary, and professional development opportunities align with your personal goals, values, and skillset? Which of these areas, if any, do you need to improve to become a successful candidate?

Alastair McCapra

Company: The Chartered Institute of Public Relations
Position: CEO

Odds are, if you are studying communication, you may like writing and social media. Use that to your advantage! McCapra advises from the first day of college, start posting on social media or writing a blog to get yourself out there and gain practice for your future career ("7 Industry Experts", 2017). Employers love to see a blog that's well established, and you can add your blog statistics to your portfolio to prove how well you engage your readers. Once more, as you make connections in the industry, consider putting your own content out there through PR contacts, and focus on making your own voice heard. The more you create and post content, the more you will get a sense of your own voice and become confident in who you are as a writer, which will help you define your place in the communications industry. It is never too early to start!

Katie Harrington, "7 Industry Experts Give Their Top Tips for Public Relations Graduates, " http://katie-harrington.ie/312-2/. Copyright © by Katie Harrington.

> **EXERCISE 8.6**
> **Prompts for Action**
>
> 1. What resources or tools do PR professionals use to do their job? How does this role align with your desired career? How can the resources and tools be used benefit you in your creation of a portfolio or resume? What benefits do you see to utilizing PR tools, resources, and tactics in your desired career, if any?
>
> 2. Develop a strategy for using social media for connecting with professionals. Use the list of podcasts to follow from an earlier chapter. Revisit the earlier chapter in which developing a social media plan was discussed. Remember the personal brand you are developing. Use social media to showcase the brand that you are.

Charlie Terenzio

Company: Newswire
Position: Public relations strategist

Terenzio advises that every time you start a new job, be it an internship or a professional position, make a list of what you want to get out of your time in that role and what you hope to accomplish there (Forbes, 2019). Having a clear objective will keep you from being distracted or wasting the precious time you have in your new role. Each job we have teaches us something about the industry, ourselves, and how to interact with others. Capitalize on that by beginning as you mean to go on! Have your plan, and review it every so often to make sure it's still applicable and you're on the right track.

> **EXERCISE 8.7**
> **Prompts for Action**
>
> 1. At the start of each semester, take time to develop a strategy to achieve your objectives. I find it helpful to consider a theme for each semester. For example, maybe this is the semester for oral communication. You may focus on using class presentations as an opportunity to develop new presentation tactics. Maybe you will use Canva instead of PowerPoint or look for other ways to present, such as in the community.
>
> 2. What is your aspirational job and organization? Learn the career path of current employees therein.

IMG 8.2

Paul Rhynard

Company: Shawn Douglas
Position: VP of operations

By the time you are done, you will likely have paid a fair amount of money for your college degree learning the theories of communication. A lot of industry leaders will tell you to throw all those theories out the moment you graduate, but that is not a great way to approach your new job. Rhynard notes, theory and practice inform each other and make you better at communicating ("7 Industry Experts," 2017). Do not sacrifice one for the other, no matter what anyone tells you. Knowing that the theory will help you in the long run will also improve your attitude while you're in college having to memorize all that information, too.

CHAPTER 8 Industry Advice   143

EXERCISE 8.8
Prompts for Action

1. Keep a log of theories you are learning in class that make the most sense to you. Add notes about how you could apply the theories to issues or problems in your intended career.

2. Find at least one opportunity to apply a theory in practice each semester. Look for student organizations, community service, part-time jobs, and so on that have a project you could tackle. Tackle the project using a theory. Keep notes, and remember to list it on your resume.

TOOLS FOR THINKING ABOUT ADVICE FROM THE INDUSTRY

McKinsey Global Institute (2021): *The Future of Work After COVID-19*

This report provides a discussion on how the COVID-19 pandemic has made lasting changes on work. You will be entering your career in a post-pandemic era. It is vital that you understand the new meaning of work.

WATCH AT https://www.mckinsey.com/featured-insights/future-of-work/the-future-of-work-after-covid-19

Janice Endresen (2020): "COVID-19's Impact on Work, Workers, and the Workplace of the Future"

This article published by Cornell University discusses the impact of the COVID-19 pandemic on work. Experts share their experiences of how a worldwide event has disrupted work.

WATCH AT https://business.cornell.edu/hub/2020/09/25/covid-19s-impact-work-workers-workplace-future/

(continued ...)

Neal Schaffer (2022): "What Do I Put in My LinkedIn Profile If I Am a College Student?"

Industry leaders advise that you network and build connections with those in your industry. This LinkedIn article provides tools for creating a profile that works while you are a college student.

WATCH AT https://nealschaffer.com/linkedin-profile-students/

CREDITS

IMG 8.1: Copyright © 2013 Depositphotos/pressmaster.
IMG 8.2: Copyright © 2015 Depositphotos/DavidArts.

Part III

FROM INTERNSHIP TO EMPLOYMENT

CHAPTER 9

Finding and Preparing for Your Internship

Internships emphasize students' experience as a member of the work force in a specific field or industry. Students take on roles as organizational members, allowing them to explore firsthand what a specific career or industry involves. It is one of the first opportunities to determine if the career, position, and field aligns with your interests, values, and skills. During an internship, the responsibility shifts to the student. It is not unlike your responsibility in the classroom, yet sometimes it may be less forgiving. Supervisors have expectations for students to take on this role as an organizational member, even if temporary. Your learning will be the direct result of participatory, engaged tasks. Internships allow you to have control of your learning and select what is important to learn. You will have a chance to check perception and connect your classroom learning within the field. You will also be able to apply theories in the field. You will be active in your education, maybe more than you ever have been to date.

You may be wondering what the advantages of completing an internship are—there are several. First, your internship experience may lead to employment. You may be able to secure a part-time job after your internship is completed, which will provide you with needed experience in field. The experience may also lead to your first job after graduation. A high percentage of internships lead to employment, either directly with the company or via the supervisor's network. It is important not to discount the importance an internship may have on your future employability.

Second, an internship will help you stand out from your competition. Internships can fast-track your preparation for the business world. I encourage you to take risks in the type of internship you pursue. Take this opportunity to aim for internships with the companies top in your specific field. Select prospective site supervisors who are your aspirational mentor. Dream big. For example, ABC News in New York City has an internship program. An option for housing is provided to interns through a first-come, first serve application process. If you are interested in TV journalism, an internship at the national level will help you stand out. For example, if you want to be in radio, look at iHeart Media for internships or CMT music in Nashville. If you have to stay local, then look for the strongest internship experience you can find locally. Internships will help you stand out, but the burden and responsibility will fall directly at your feet. You will have to perform in your internship to reap the benefits. Internships will allow you to refine skills and gain new ones.

Another advantage of completing an internship is it can help you network in your chosen profession. You will want to make sure you have two things ready prior to starting your internship: business cards and an active LinkedIn account. Many university print shops will create business cards for students. If your university does not, you can easily create business cards on your own or print them directly from your computer; you will want to purchase business card paper for this. You may also use an inexpensive service to have cards professionally printed, such as VistaPrint. LinkedIn will help you manage and make the most of your connections. You will want to develop a habit of asking people if they would mind if you connected with them on LinkedIn. Also, create a habit of sending requests immediately after meeting the person. Some of the best internships for those who are uncertain of their aspirational career are with the local chamber of commerce. Chamber of commerce offices are charged with the task of connecting with local businesses. Nearly all of them have weekly breakfasts or lunches, and interns are often invited to attend the meetings. This is an amazing opportunity to meet business leaders in your community.

Several years ago I had a student who interned a chamber of commerce. Not only did she meet fantastic business leaders, but she had them competing for her after graduation. You read that right. She had four job offers from people she met while interning at the chamber of commerce. She was able to use this to her advantage and select the right job for her. And by the way, the position she chose was one specifically created for her. The opportunity to research and explore potential careers is another advantage of internships; your research will be experiential. One of the most important advantages of internships is that you will be able to determine if the field or career is a good fit for you. The result of this may change your career focus. Adjusting your career focus is a perfectly fine result of an internship. You will have the support of your faculty and academic advisor to manage the adjustment. Internships will foster and encourage personal growth as well as help you build self-confidence in new settings.

Experiential Learning

Figure 9.1 shows the **experiential learning** model. Internships are considered an activity of experiential learning. You will see the components of this type of learning are concrete experience, reflective observation, abstract conceptualization, and active experimentation. An example of **concrete experience** is completing an assignment at your internship. It adds to your portfolio. An example of **reflective observation** is thinking about the assignment you completed in the internship during a coffee break or while driving home. The **abstract conceptualization** of the assignment is when you form ideas and theories about the completed or ongoing assignment. You will be engaging in active experimentation when you test the theories learned in the classroom by asking coworkers, friends, and faculty about your ideas and theories. Internships are an engaged process of connecting the academic with the work world. Throughout the internship you must be active in the learning process; you must be disciplined. You also will need to determine what you want to learn and how much. This usually happens before the internship starts. Most communication departments will require you to develop a learning contract that outlines about four **learning objectives** for your internship. You will create learning objectives, which are statements about what you want to learn. These will become your initial learning objectives. You should work with your faculty to evaluate your learning objectives to determine if they are realistic. Refine the statements as needed before finalizing them. Determine how you will know if and when you achieve the learning objectives. It is suggested that you include these in your learning contact or internship paperwork. Remember that having the official learning objectives at the start of the experience is not the end of it. Your attitude and approach throughout the internship will demonstrate how much you want to learn and what about. You will also will be evaluating your own work and learning, not just your site supervisor and faculty. It is common that students are required to write a self-reflection paper at the end of the internship.

Now that we have discussed experiential learning and learning objectives, you will have a chance to practice writing learning objectives for your internship. Up to this point, learning objectives have been imposed on you in your courses. You received a syllabus at the start of the semester that listed several learning objectives for the class. It is your turn, most likely in consultation with your faculty, to determine what the objectives adding to your learning will be.

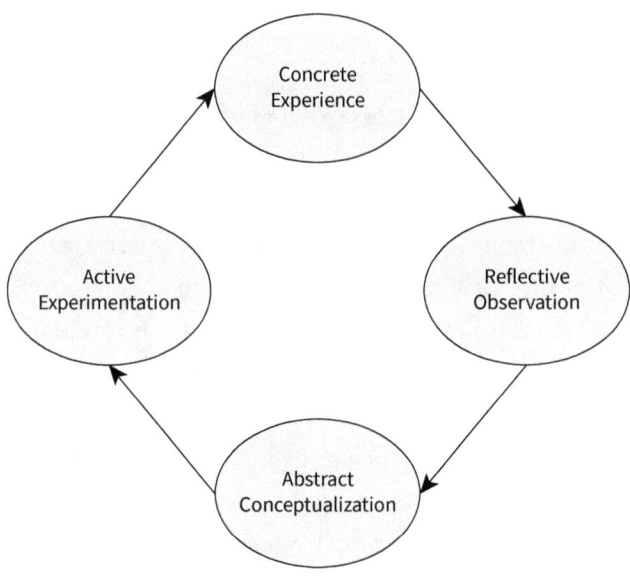

FIGURE 9.1 Experiential Learning

EXERCISE 9.1
Writing Learning Objectives for Your Internship

There are three types of learning objectives fitting for an internship: academic, professional, and personal. This exercise will have you write several of each kind. In practice, it is suggested that you speak with your faculty or academic advisor when developing objectives for your actual internship:

- **Academic:** A statement that measures what and how you are planning to apply the concepts or theories of your major and/or acquiring new knowledge and understanding of your major.
    - *Example*: Learn applications of effective meeting management.
    - *Example*: Apply principles for effective communication to respond to customer complaints.

What are your Academic objectives? Try writing two academic objectives for your future internship.

_____
_____
_____
_____

(continued ...)

- **Professional:** A statement that measures what and how you are planning to develop skills related to your major or career as well as transferable skills.
  - *Example*: Make professional contacts who can help me with my job search after graduation.
  - *Example*: Identify visual merchandising practices.

What are your Professional objectives? Try writing two professional objectives for your future internship.

_____

_____

_____

_____

- **Personal:** A statement that measures what and how you seek to develop that are not directly academic or professional in nature for personal development. Examples might include self-awareness, self-confidence, and appreciation for diversity.
  - *Example*: Determine if working for a radio station is an appropriate career goal for me.
  - *Example*: Develop my potential as a facilitator in group meetings.

What are your personal objectives? Try writing two personal objectives for your future internship.

_____

_____

_____

_____

The Nature of Internships

Understanding the nature of internships and the requirements of your communication program will help focus your search for internships. Internships are offered across different type of organizations, including those big and small, across all industries, obviously communication-related as well as not as obviously, and via face-to-face or virtual communication. Internships are offered locally, regionally, nationally, and internationally. Keep your mind open to all types of internships, unless you are restricted by your program. When looking for internships, never discount the opportunities small businesses present. Generally, these are unpaid, but they might offer more hands-on experience than internships at large organizations.

It important to choose internships that will enhance your learning experience and not just apply for any open internship you come across. In the post COVID-19 era, finding face-to-face internship might be challenging. The good news is that many organizations are open to virtual or telecommuting internship opportunities. Remember that "different" does not equate to "bad" or "less than." Different is an opportunity. Embrace the opportunity to explore innovative ways to complete an internship and add work experience to your resume. It's not only important to find the best internship for you and your goals for the future, but it is also an opportunity to learn outside of the classroom, regardless of the field or location. Remember that throughout the experience of the internship if you do not feel challenges, seek out more projects and assignments with your supervisor.

The first thing you need to do before finding an internship is consider your own qualifications that your major in communication provide as well as any working experience and your skills and interests. It is helpful to use the self-analyses in this book to help find the right kind of internship for you. Also be certain to have the requirements of your communication program at your side when starting to search for an internship.

Finding Your Internship

You should start your search for an internship 6–9 months in advance. Certain industries and organizations have early deadlines. It is not uncommon for communication internships with professional sports teams to have a yearlong, or longer, process. Broadcasting jobs with national news agencies also have an extended process for applying for an internship. There are different methods for searching for internships, including searching the internet, prospecting, networking, attending career fairs, and browsing your university's job listings or Handshake. Handshake is similar to LinkedIn but used by universities. Students can create a profile on Handshake and search and apply for internships and jobs. Employers can post open positions and recruit directly from a university's Handshake account. It is recommended that you reach out to your university's career services to see if Handshake is being used. The more you use Handshake the greater chance your profile will be seen by prospective employers (visit joinhandshake.com to create an account).

It is probably the most obvious way to start your search for that life-changing internship with the internet. The internet is your greatest resource in finding an internship. You can begin by you using your favorite search engine and keywords related to the type of internship you are seeking. Use the results to explore the posted internships. Be aware of fraudulent internship advertisements. After doing a general search you will want to use some specific and helpful sites to look for an internship. Table 9.1 provides a list of a good sites to search for internships.

As you explore the different websites there are few things you should do. First, I recommend keeping a file on your computer or a notebook to write all your searches and the key words you used. I would recommend you list the website used, date each entry, and list the keywords used during the search. Capture the results as an action list. Set up a table with four columns: the company's name, the name of the internship position, the action or next step, and an update. Use this table to capture all the places you are looking into and applying. Update it as you advance through the process of submitting an application and as you, hopefully, advance through the application and hiring process. Having such organized notes will help you stay on track and moving forward. It will also eliminate wasting time repeating steps or not remembering if you looked at a particular internship. Another advantage of using this approach is having something to show your faculty or academic advisor. When you find a site that is useful, sign up for notifications. It is helpful to receive an email with new internship advertisements that match your search criteria; this will save you the time of checking the website each day.

TABLE 9.1   Internet Sources for Searching for an Internship

Website	Key Features
LinkedIn	<ul><li>Search box</li><li>Can refine search</li><li>Networking with alumni</li><li>Offers analytics</li><li>Shows connections associated with companies</li></ul>
Glassdoor	<ul><li>Viewing job salaries</li><li>Reading company reviews</li><li>Reading descriptions of job interviews</li></ul>
Internship.com	<ul><li>Owned by Chegg</li><li>Its "who" button lets you see which of your Facebook friends have a connection to a company</li></ul>

(continued ...)

Website	Key Features
Intermatch.com	- Specializes in internships and entry-level jobs less than two years after graduation
YouTern	- Offers mentorship - Connects would-be interns using social media tools like Twitter
Idealist	- A nonprofit organization
Global Experiences	- Offers international internships, which the inter pays for. Some universities pick up the tab - Students must apply, but once accepted, placement is guaranteed
CareerConnections	- Powered by Facebook - Can receive notifications
AngelList	- Lists startup companies' internship postings - Can receive notifications
The Muse	- Offers career coaching for a fee - Lists national and international internships (and jobs) - Can receive notifications
Indeed	- Can receive notifications
Wayup.com	- Paid internships - Startups and Fortune 500 companies - Prides itself on communication within 24 hours once applications have been submitted

Prospecting is one method for looking for suitable internships. Note that not all organizations advertise for interns, but that does not mean they don't need or want them. By approaching companies you might have more ability to shape your own internship. Since prospecting requires you to approach organizations that are not advertising for interns, there may be less competition for the position. Prospecting for internships gives you the ability to target organizations you value, and it may even streamline the search for an internship process.

Networking is another great method to use to locate a suitable internship. It is not unusual that about 80% of openings are never advertised; therefore, networking is an important strategy for learning about possibilities. It is similar to prospecting, except you rely on your established network and their network. Announce your internship search to everyone you know to develop a list of contacts and leads. Connect with people, and build relationships. Remember you are networking all the time. Ask questions, learn about other people, and let them know about you. Take interest in the jobs of others. Remember Aunt Susan, who as an interesting job with ESPN. She might be helpful connecting you to the right person to explore opportunities. It is a good idea to set networking goals for yourself. Make it a priority throughout college, not just before needing an internship. It is key that you develop a 30-second pitch—an elevator pitch. When networking, you have to be prepared to pitch yourself.

> **EXERCISE 9.2**
> **Developing Your 30-Second Elevator Pitch**
>
> Use the following image to plan your 30-second elevator pitch to use when you are networking and are looking for an internship or a job. Once you have it planned, it is very helpful to record your elevator pitch. Practice it. Use the principles of effective speech you learned throughout your communication program. Practice not speaking too fast and being conversational in tone.

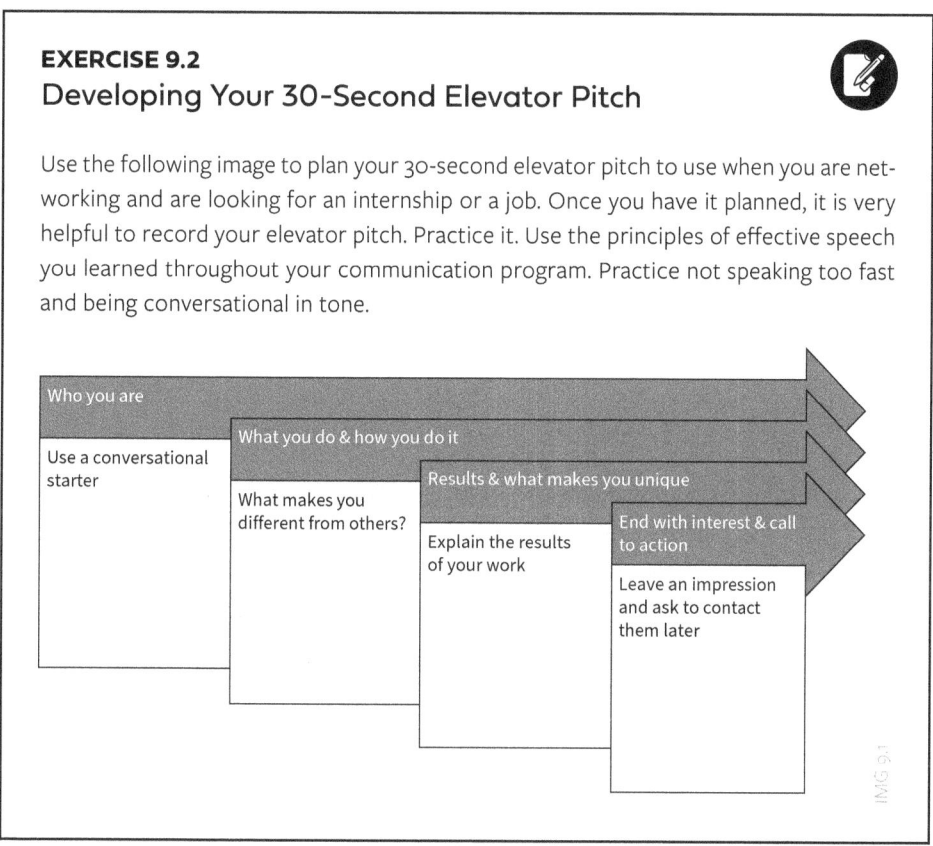

Career fairs are another place to look for internships. Attend internships and job fairs to connect with recruiters. It is really never too early to start attending career fairs. It is important to get familiar with the resources available, and it is a great way to research. Before attending a fair you should research employers attending the fair. Most fairs will publish a list of companies and organizations that will be recruiting during the fair. Research the attendees, and make a plan of action. You will most likely have limited time, so create a strategy for how you will manage the fair. Think ahead about what you are going to wear. It is expected that you will be wearing appropriate interview attire. Dressing professionally will empower you and help you decide on the impression you will make. If you don't have a suit, check out local consignment shops. You will be amazed the high-quality clothes you may find. Also, check with your university. I know many, like Purdue University (Purdue University, 2022), have career closets, which offer professional clothing for free to students. If these two options are not available, check with the local community. Many communities have dress for success programs that provide interview clothing to those who do not have resources to otherwise get suits. I would recommend contacting the local chamber of commerce, as they will be able to direct you to resources. Bring copies of your polished resume and business cards. Be sure to follow up on leads and networking opportunities.

Check with your university's career services. They usually have job listings and many use Handshake. Take advantage of career services. The staff work hard to build a vast network of employers looking to work with your university's students. That is you! You may be able to post a resume, so employers can find you.

Preparing for Your Internship

Now that you have some leads on internships it is important to focus on other ways to prepare for internships. Preparing for an internship is very important, especially if it's your first one. The first step in preparing for an internship is to have a resume that is good enough to warrant an interview. As a communication major you are aware of the importance of being persuasive to receive the action you are seeking. In the case of resume, this written document is a tool to persuade the recruiter or employer to offer you an interview. With jobs and internships becoming more and more competitive, it's a challenge to stand out. One key way to make a resume stand out from others is to write about past experiences in a way that enhances your current career goals. When writing a resume or being interviewed, it is important that you translate your experiences into skills that are desired for the target internship. Using keywords the company is looking for in their employees is also important. Remember the earlier exercises you completed, giving you experience with identifying skills, interests, and alignment with the company's mission statement. Your resume should clearly highlight any achievements you have accomplished at your previous employment that showcase your skills in action. Organize your work history to display situations and tasks you faced and how you handled them. Quantifying experience into numbers, like guests helped, products sold, or money raised, also helps make your resume stand out. It also helps to have a resume that looks different than the others. Using different design features can definitely help your resume "pop" against the others and get the recruiters' attention. Be sure to use the resources at your university, and ask your faculty to review and provide feedback on your resume prior submitting job applications.

While cover letters aren't always required, they help separate your application from others. A cover letter is your first opportunity to persuade the employer you are a good fit for the position and the organization. The cover letter should be concise but give the employer a sense of your work ethic, qualifications, and enthusiasm to work for the company.

While resumes and cover letters are an important first step for preparing for an internship, it is simply a tool to get you to the next phase: the interview. Most employers don't spend much time looking at resumes. Once basic qualifications are met, employers are looking to see what kind of person you are, and personality can't be easily translated through a piece of paper. Having a link to your video cover letter or resume added to your written cover letter and resume can aid the employer in seeing more of you and how you might fit with the company. Always be certain to ask your faculty if including such links is appropriate for the specific internships for which you are applying.

A part of preparing for an internship is preparing for an interview. Many companies will weed out potential applicants based on their resume alone and will follow up with an interview only for those candidates they saw promise in. Preparing for an interview includes things like deciding what to wear and preparing for questions an interviewer might ask. It is also important to know things about the company, like who they are, what they do, their mission statement and values, important figureheads in the company, and any recent accomplishments they have had. It's also important for you to come to the interview with questions of your own that will allow you to get a better feel for what you will be doing and how you will fit in. Your questions will show you are engaged and interested.

It is also key to be confident and positive during an interview. Self-confidence is part of selling yourself, and employers are looking for confidence. It is important to do your homework and prepare for the internship interview. Use the resources your department and university provides. Look up commonly asked questions during an internship interview. It is standard to arrive roughly 10 minutes early to the interview. Etiquette is also important and might help you stand out from your competition to the interviewer. It is important to stay off all electronic devices as you wait for your interview to start as well as throughout the interview. The only exception will be to show your digital portfolio. I suggest bringing a small laptop or iPad. Hoovering over a small phone to look at your portfolio is not appealing.

Be sure to thank the interview for their time, and ask for a business card. After the interview, follow up with a phone call or a letter. The timing of this should be within two days of the interview. The advantage of the follow-up is not only to showcase your stellar etiquette or writing skills, but it also reminds the interviewer of your application well after the interview was completed.

EXERCISE 9.3
Preparing for Common Interview Questions

The following list contains some of the most common questions asked during an interview for a college internship. Review each one, and make notes on how you might answer.

1. Why are you interested in the internship or the company?
2. Why do you want to work in this industry?
3. Where do you see yourself after graduation?
4. What skills do you hope to gain during this internship?
5. What is the best team you have worked with? What made it the best team?
6. Tell me about a time you took initiative. What was the result?
7. Describe a project you completed. What went well? What would you have done differently?
8. Tell me about when you had to learn something new.
9. Talk about an accomplishment you that you are most proud of. Why?
10. Do you have questions for me?

SPOTLIGHT ON COMMUNICATION
Narrative Theory

The thought that everyone is essentially a storyteller is known as narrative theory. Some of the aspects of this theory are that reality is socially constructed and that it is influence by communication. Personal narratives help us maintain as well as organize our own reality. I won't be going into the details of this theory in this text, but I highlight it because it provides food for thought regarding how to approach your internship, especially the interview. It is important that the interview is a time to share your narrative—your story. The interview is exactly the time you are shaping and constructing reality. Storytelling is one of first forms of communication, and it is considered universal. According to narrative theory stories are how we approach our social world and how we make decisions and act. If there is no objective reality, your communication and telling of your story may influence how the interviewer views you. When considering

(continued ...)

how you will present yourself and your personal brand integrate impactful stories that showcase your experience, skills, and overall fit for the position. When selecting stories to share during an interview be sure they match your personal brand. Also, know your audience. If your interview was with members of the same sorority or fraternity you were in, you can use that to your advantage by selecting a story that might be shared with the interviewer. Have several different stories prepared. Practice, and take time to prepare your story.

TOOLS FOR GETTING AN INTERNSHIP

By searching the internet, you can find internship handbooks for students on university websites. Doing some research you will find it valuable to learn what other universities advise and require of their students. Consider how you might use the information you find to further enrich your internship experience.

Polk State College Internship Handbook

WATCH AT https://www.polk.edu/wp-content/uploads/INTERNSHIP-HANDBOOK-092015-Rev1.pdf

CUNY Internship Programs Intern Handbook

WATCH AT https://www.cuny.edu/wp-content/uploads/sites/4/media-assets/CIP_Intern_Handbook.pdf

University of South Florida Internship Handbook

WATCH AT https://www.usf.edu/career-services/documents/employers/internship-handbook.pdf

KEY TERMS

abstract conceptualization: The abstract conceptualization of the assignment is when you form ideas and theories about the completed or ongoing assignment.

concrete experience: Experiential learning activities that provide tangible experience represented by demonstrable skills.

experiential learning: A type of learning that involves concrete experience, reflective observation, abstract conceptualization, and active experimentation.

learning objectives: Statements about what a person will or wants to learn.

reflective observation: Reflective observation is processes information about an experience.

CHAPTER 10

Top 10 "Must Dos" During Your Internship

Completing an internship could potentially increase your chance of employment straight out of college. Internships are key to extending your education and connecting it to the work economy. Communication majors benefit from internships because there are so many diverse jobs and careers that employ communication majors. It is important for you to gain more exposure to the various types of jobs and careers you pursue after graduation. An internship is only as valuable as you are successful in making a positive impression on those you work with, especially your site supervisor. To be successful in your internship and beyond there are several "must dos" during your internship. This chapter discusses ten "must dos," or goals, and tactics for achieving them.

As mentioned in the previous chapter, internships emphasize students' experience as a member of the work force in a specific field or industry. Since you will be afforded the opportunity to become an organizational member for the duration of the internship, this opportunity reminds me of when my family and I went on vacation during the winter to the mountains and stayed in a log home. I dreamt of owning a log home up on a mountain close to the ski resorts for years. This vacation was my chance to become a resident of a mountain community. I did not own the home. This is just like an internship: You don't have a full-time job with the company; however, you get to enter the building each day and feel connected to the company and its employees, like I took on the role of caretaker of the home during my stay. Many of the activities I did felt like home ownership. I had to shovel snow, deal with the electric company when a snowstorm knocked out the power for days, and take out the trash. OK, these don't sound too appealing, but I also got to go skiing, walk my dogs in the snow, make a fire in the fireplace, gaze at the amazing views, and meet the neighbors. Internships are very similar to renting a home during a vacation. You get a chance to see both the positive and negative sides of the job and organization. I learned from my vacation that if I ever have the chance to purchase a log home in the mountains I will investigate how the roads are maintained on the mountain and will definitely need a generator for when we lose power. You too will come away from your internship with a better idea of what you require in a job, employer, and company.

Since many internships lead to employment after graduation you need to approach the internship seriously and professionally. As we review some of the most important things to do during your internship, many might appear to be common sense, yet they are often pitfalls for students. Each recommendation is discussed along with specific tactics and best practices for achieving the goal. The top things you must successfully achieve while interning include the following:

- Make a first impression.
- Make connections.
- Be professional.
- Have learning objectives.
- Ask questions.
- Find opportunities to shine.
- Ask for feedback.
- Take notes.
- Adapt to the business culture.
- Explore.

Make a First Impression

Now that you got the internship it is important to manage the impression others have of you. For most supervisors they will move past the first impressions made during the interview process for interns. When you arrive for your first day of interning, you are given the opportunity make an everlasting impression on your coworkers and superiors. How can you make the most of this opportunity? Making a great first impression isn't as hard as it sounds. There are some reliable ingredients for putting your best foot forward. These ingredients include being prepared, being confident, having a positive attitude, arriving early, and introducing yourself to others. Let's take a closer look at each of these ingredients.

It has never been more important to be prepared when starting your internship and remaining prepared throughout it. Note that many employers are not as forgiving as some of your faculty have been when you fall short in preparing for class. From the very first day, be prepared and well researched. As a student of communication, recognize that being prepared is one of the most persuasive messages you provide your employers and colleagues. When I reflect on my over two decades' worth of conversations with site supervisors, they always discuss students' preparation—for the good or for the bad. Chances are your faculty overseeing your internship will be using your site supervisor's evaluation to determine your course grade for the internship. If you fall short with your supervisor you may be hurting your chances to truly benefit from the internship as well as earning your desired grade in the course. One tactic for being prepared is studying the organizational chart; learn the chain of command, and memorize it. This will help you understand the structure of the company as well as who your site supervisor reports to. Another tactic is to come prepared understanding the company's mission statement and values. Work to embody both each and every day. Also, come prepared with a list of questions. You should not come charging in the first day, rambling off each and every question you have. Rather, you will find it handy to have a list of preplanned questions to use as conversation starters to show interest in projects and generally learn more about the job, company, and industry. Just like we spoke about earlier, have your questions represent each of the three kinds of questions. You will soon discover that these questions enrich your learning experience and show your supervisor and colleagues you are genuinely interested in the company and job. Manage the impression others form of you by being engaged and excited about the work. It's important to ask questions and carry a notebook around to record important information about why you should be hired for a full-time position.

EXERCISE 10.1
Making a Positive First Impression

Jackie Fern, a television journalist, offers three easy steps to make a positive first impression at your internship, based on the horror stories from her interning days at CNN, NY1, and AC 360. Watch this short video for examples of how to manage your impression: https://www.youtube.com/watch?v=I78kYyqw_IM.

Discuss some specific tips and tactics offered in the video.

_____
_____
_____
_____

In addition to being prepared it is important to present yourself as being confident. Often, this is harder than it sounds. Being confident as an intern while entering a company is tricky. Confidence can be exuded through communication, in small and big ways. Dress for the job you want, not the one you have. It is thought that that way you dress influences the way your behave. It is okay is wear dress clothes that are a tad uncomfortable; it will remind you throughout the day that you are taking on a new and different role. While you are in the workplace, you are no longer a student. Beyond just dressing for the internship you should practice smiling. There is nothing more welcoming that seeing someone smile. You will find that others are more likely to interact with you, and you will gain confidence knowing you are prepared and informed about the internship, supervisor, and company. Don't apologize for your lack of knowledge or skills; rather, own it, and focus on communicating your eagerness to learn and do your homework to catch up.

Related to being confident is having a positive attitude. You will find that a positive attitude goes a long way and communicates a lot of information to those around you. The fact is people like being around happy people. If you are able to bring light into the workplace, you will be remembered for being pleasant to work with. There are some tactics for having a positive attitude to keep in mind. First, be sure you get a good night's rest. Sleep has magical effects on attitude. On the eve of internship workdays, skip the late nights, and get some rest. Avoid complaining in the workplace as well as outside of the workplace. As communication majors you know the power of negative messages and their influence on our internal dialogue. Don't only not complain, but have a solution orientation toward problems. This means when problems arise, and they most likely will, rather than complain, develop the instinct to think about possible solutions. You will find this puts you more in control and reinforces a positive attitude.

The final two ingredients for creating a good first impression are arriving early and introducing yourself to others. Internships are not a place for tardiness or absences. Too often I hear from site supervisors about student interns being late, leaving early, or being absent. It is a key lesson to learn that businesses do not operate on university time. Your spring break does not entitle you days off from the workplace. I highly recommend you speak about any days off you need before accepting the internship. Plan to arrive to the workplace at least 10 minutes early. Take this opportunity to get settled in your space and greet colleagues. If you need to be late, be sure to communicate this as early as possible. Remember that just because you communicate being late or absent does not mean your supervisor will not "hold it against you." I remember a site supervisor telling me about an intern who was late several times due to not having reliable transportation, resulting in breakdowns. Even though your car breaking down seems like a good reason for being late or missing work altogether, it is not seen that way by many supervisors. Be mindful of a professional.

The final ingredient for creating a fabulous impression is introducing yourself to others. We will talk about networking and building relationship next, but it is worth mentioning here that as you start your internship career you want to create the habit of introducing yourself and greeting others throughout your workday. There is a scene in an old movie, *Working Girl* (Nichols, 1988), in which a younger professional steps into the elevator with the CEO of the company. The employee represents everything we have discussed, and she was ready to seize the opportunity to present an idea to the CEO. I am not suggesting you come on as strong, but it is wise to make the most of every opportunity you are given. When you see someone struggling with a pile of papers and opening the door, help, and open the door. Such a gesture communicates volumes. It shows you are friendly, helpful, considerate, observant, and so many other things. You want people leaving an interaction with you thinking, "What a great intern." The ultimate goal of a successful internship is to be missed when your time is over. You want your colleagues and supervisor to think that they need you to stay—permanently!

Make Connections

Building a professional web of people who can assist you in starting your career is very important. Communication majors are expected to be excellent networkers; both go hand-and-hand. Effective networking is more than collecting business cards or LinkedIn connections; rather, it is important to attend to each connection and build a relationship with each person. Never send a request to connect on LinkedIn without a personal note. Remind the person how you met, and add a sentiment of why you value being connected. As a student, I would encourage you to create a process for paying attention to connections on LinkedIn. For example, comment on posts your connections write. Send notes of congratulations around work anniversaries and promotions that are noted on LinkedIn. If you notice an article of interest, request to meet up in person or via Zoom to learn more. Show interest in the professional lives of your connections. Another recommendation is to be armed with a list of informational questions to learn more about someone you meet. This is as important when starting your career just as it is later in your career. Never stop wanting to learn about others. LinkedIn is a great tool to help manage your network, but never use Facebook to build or manage your professional network. Be sure to track the individuals in your network. Set a timeline for when you will engage your network, so the connection stays strong. As an intern you should get to know your colleagues throughout the entire time at the internship. These are connections that might lead to future employment.

> **SPOTLIGHT ON COMMUNICATION**
> **Impression Management**
>
> Think for a second about the decisions you made this morning when getting dressed. You most likely took several things into consideration when dressing. First, you might have looked at what you had that was clean. Next, you might have considered the context you would be in for the day. Maybe you would be at work, or perhaps you

(continued ...)

were traveling for business; regardless, the context played a role in determining the appropriate attire. Another factor you might have considered was how comfortable the clothes were. Just like getting dressed, we make decisions about our communication, both verbal and nonverbal. Our communication reflects who we are to others. The research that examines how we use communication to influence how others look at us is called impression management.

Impression management is the process of creating the image of yourself that is perceived by others. This process includes editing, packaging, and communicating information to others. Impression management is a key interpersonal process that is goal directed. We communicate in such a way to influence how others see us. Impression management is sometimes referred to as self-presentation. Leary and Kowalski (1990) assert that impression management may or may not include authentic presentation. Further, Goffman (1959) in his book, *The Presentation of Self in Everyday Life*, argues that impression management is more than just influencing how you are treated by others but is an essential part of social interaction.

There are several tactics we use to manage others' impression of us. Conformity is one tactic in which you adapt your communication to match those around you. You recognize the norms associated with the context you are communicating in, and you behave within the accepted norms. When you notice your behavior is not within the norms, you may offer an excuse. An excuse is the second type of impression management tactic. Alternatively, you may offer an apology instead of an excuse. Apologies can be effective at managing and repairing the impression you make on others. The fourth tactic is using self-promotion to boost the impression you make. One does need to self-promote with caution because there is a ceiling. A ceiling refers to the amount of self-promotion that is not considered excessive. Bragging often hinders or harms your impression with others. Rather than boosting yourself, you may choose to flatter others as an attempt to control the impression you make on others. The next tactic is doing favors for others. One must be careful of the context when offering to do favors. For example, one should cautious in the workplace, as you do not want the favor to be misinterpreted as a bribe. The final two tactics for impression management include associations and opinion conformity. Associations refers to using your network to improve others' view of you. The idea behind this tactic is that people will think of you differently if you are surround by important or influential people. We discussed earlier that conformity is when you change your behavior to fit the norms of the context. Opinion conformity is similar, except it means striving to hold the same opinion as others with whom you are seeking to make a favorable impression. With all the tactics, you must be aware of the people you are hoping to impress and the communication behaviors they value. It is important that they align with your personal values. Using the tactics to manipulate is not a positive decision and may have the reverse effect.

Understanding the concept that importance of the impressions you make on those you work with or hope to work with is vital to gaining entry into the workplace. When building your network, looking for an internship, and looking for a job, you will want to create positive impressions of others. When appropriate, use some of the tactics to help form impressions or even repair an impression if a bad one was formed.

> **EXERCISE 10.2**
> **Making the Most of Internships**
>
> Watch the following video available on YouTube: "Internships & Networking" by NatpeEd (2008), in which television journalism professionals share insight on making the most of internships: https://www.youtube.com/watch?v=Lql7Iwf7M6A.
>
>
>
> Record some advice you took from the video:
> _____
> _____
> _____
> _____

Be Professional

An internship is only useful if it is a positive experience for you and your site. You will want to work toward becoming a part of the organization. As an intern the reality is you have one foot in the company and one foot in the university. You are walking in two worlds. A mistake many interns make is mixing up the two worlds, bringing in the expectations of faculty into the workplace. Supervisors will expect professional behavior. They do not want to see you as anything other than an employee. Don't disappoint them by being viewed as a student. Engage your colleagues. Participate in company events you are invited to attend. Learn the rules that govern employees' behavior, both implicit and explicit.

> **EXERCISE 10.3**
> **Becoming a Trusted Member of an Organization**
>
> Lauren Berger (2017) offers suggestions for five things you can do to during your internship. Watch her brief video, "5 Ways to Be a Great Intern! | The Intern Queen," for insight into what you can do to increase your chances of becoming a trusted member of the organization as an intern: https://www.youtube.com/watch?v=VNSe2kcqO9w.

(continued ...)

What five tips did you hear in the video? Write them below in order of which you believe are most important for your internship:

_____
_____
_____
_____

Have Learning Objectives

It is important to challenge yourself to learn new skills. In the previous chapter you learned how to write learning objectives for your internship. Don't lose sight of your learning objectives. Ideally, these objectives were agreed upon by the site supervisor and will provide the structure for the internship. It is a great idea to identify smaller goals for skill development each week. Use these smaller goals to get the most from your experience. Look at job advertisements for open full-time positions with the company and other similar companies. Be mindful of the lists of required skills and preferred skills. How are you gaining experience in each of the areas? Add skills you gain to your resume before you forget. It is also a great idea to start a folder on your computer and keep a running list of descriptions of projects, skills, and experiences. You will rely on these memories as you prepare for interviews. Many employers favor asking open-ended, experience-based questions. An effective response will include specific examples from your work experience. Focus on gathering experience with technical skills, relational skills, time-management skills, and initiative.

EXERCISE 10.4
Challenging Yourself

In this brief video from Google Students (2013), "Meet Alyx, a Google Sales Intern," listen to a Google intern share her story about how to challenge yourself during an internship: https://www.youtube.com/watch?v=cP2fsFpAcig.

(continued ...)

Discuss how Aleyx challenged herself while at Google:

_____
_____
_____
_____

Brainstorm different ways you could challenge yourself in your internship:

_____
_____
_____
_____

Ask Questions

As a student you receive a syllabus at the start of the semester for each course. You have come to rely on it as one of the many features of student life. Once you receive the syllabus, knowing what is expected of you is fairly straightforward. Assignments are listed and described and even weighted. You know what actions will fulfill the requirements of assignments and projects. In the workplace it is not that cut and dry. It is important to show initiative and independent thinking while asking questions for clarity and interest. It is a balancing act. It is important for you to understand instructions for the tasks you will complete. Generally, there are not rubrics for assignments in the workplace. Life is not a dot-to-dot coloring book, in which you are instructed to go from one dot to the next to be successful. Instead, the workplace is filled with ambiguity. It is your job to take what is given and demonstrate your ability to be successful. It is true that many people in the workplace come to expect that their employees can anticipate what they want. Ask questions as an intern. It is important show that you care about the task and doing your best work. Apply what you learned earlier in this book about the three types of questions to ask. Be sure to vary your questions. If you just ask comprehension questions you will be demonstrating you cannot follow instructions as given the first time. You may be showing that you cannot think independently. Too many questions of comprehension will leave the impression that you need hand-holding. The other two questions, bridging and connecting, reveal more critical thinking, and as long as they are on topic, they will be viewed as positive participation in the workplace.

Remember the internship is a training ground. Most site supervisors understand that interns will have excellent skills in one area and weak skills in another. As an intern you can set the tone for receiving feedback. Feedback may be a requirement of your internship. Establish your expectation for receiving feedback throughout the internship. You may even request a conversation at the end of your second week. It is long enough for you to get used to the workplace and short enough to correct any behaviors the supervisor sees as being negative. Always as for an exit interview.

Find Opportunities to Shine

As a communication major you probably have been exposed to persuasion theory. Maybe you took an entire class on persuasion, a theory class, or public speaking. One of the basic principles of creating a message in public speaking is determining whether your intent is to inform, persuade, or maybe both. Has a faculty told you that all communication is persuasion? Why might a faculty see communication as persuasive in nature? Perhaps because when you communicate you there is a desire to want others to listen to what you are saying. Now apply this to internships. When you are an intern you are persuading your supervisor and your colleagues that you belong—that you have the skills and knowledge to fit right in. It is important that as part of your approach to persuading your supervisor and colleagues you demonstrate you are ready and able to perform than tasks not only of the internship but an entry level, full-time position. To do this you will need to find opportunities to shine. Ask for more assignments. Offer to do more work, or if appropriate work more hours. Remember that more seasoned employees and your supervisor have paid their dues to earn their positions in the organization and the industry. Respect that you will need to pay your dues too. This usually entails doing more work, taking on a variety of tasks (some you may be overqualified to do), and volunteering your time and skills. Don't misread this sentiment; I am not saying you should be taken advantage of. Your radar will go off if you have a sense that you are being taken advantage of. If you suspect this is happening, share your concern with your academic advisor or faculty internship advisor.

Another part of finding opportunities to shine is to anticipating the company or department's needs. Employ effective listening and observation skills to learn and sense what these needs are. How might you lend your time and skills to assist your supervisor or colleagues? As with almost anything, manage the balance of being a supportive and contributing employee (intern) and being dominating and over eager. Again, remember what you have learned about persuasion in your courses, and apply it to striving for a balance in how you project yourself to others in the workplace.

A final way to distinguish yourself from others and, as a result, shine is to be respectful and adhere to principles of etiquette. "Please" and "thank you" can go a long way. Showing gratitude demonstrates you are respectful of others. Avoid getting involved in office gossip. Be mindful of how you talk about others.

Take Notes

I mentioned earlier that it would be helpful to keep a folder on your computer where you store experiences from your internship. Don't stop there; keep a record of class experiences connected to your future career. You want to have a database of sorts of information to use in cover letters, resumes, and interviews. Develop a method for listing assignments; methods for completing the assignment, such as using new software or hardware; and the result of the project, including feedback from stakeholders. Many college internship courses require students to keep a journal during your internship. Be sure you keep your journal after the internship is concluded. The following table is a template for journaling.

Date (Hours Worked)	Summary of Work Tasks	Outcomes	Challenges	Keywords Related to Classes Taken

Adapt to the Business Culture

It is important to remember that as a new member of the organization you will need to adapt to the culture. This will include dressing the part by observing others and behaving in a way that aligns with others in the office. Pay attention to the explicit and implicit rules in the workplace. Explicit rules are those that are expressed, either orally or in writing. You will find explicit rules discussed in employee (or intern) handbooks. You may receive emails that include explicit rules, and sometimes the explicit rules are orally shared by a supervisor. Implicit

---

EXERCISE 10.5
Managing Organizational Culture

Watch this short video, "Interns' Take on Organizational Culture," from Elevate Experiences (2019), in which a group of interns discuss how they managed the organizational culture of their internship sites: https://www.youtube.com/watch?v=bnPI8RrCbNc.

Write some notes on recognizing and making sense of an organization's culture:
_____
_____
_____
_____

Discuss what varied in the different organizational cultures the interns discussed:
_____
_____
_____
_____

(continued ...)

> Discuss how the interns felt they could influence the organizational culture:
>
> _____
> _____
> _____
> _____

rules are not necessarily spoken or written, yet they are known by the members. Implicit rules are only known through keen observation. Be mindful to watch how employees perform their duties and tasks. Implicit rules often come into our awareness when we violate them.

Explore

The final "must do" on the list is using the internship as a reason to explore the specific industry you are interning in. Learn what others do in the office. Consider the various tasks others are responsible for. Reflect on your skillset and what you have learned and experienced throughout your internship. Look for the best match for you.

There are a couple methods that can help an intern turn an internship to a job. Interns should never be late, as it sets a negative impression about their work ethic. It's also important for the intern to seek new assignments. It's never a good look to be doing nothing. Interns should always make sure the work they are producing is perfect, even triple checking their numbers. Employers want to see competent workers. Interns should also display their seriousness and focus for their work by not being on their phone during work hours. Even if it's just a quick thirty-minute meeting, finding time to network and connect with coworkers and supervisors one on one is important!

When thinking about participating in an internship and all the behaviors that are part of being successful, you may think of salad—yes, salad. As you probably know, salads these days can be far from some lettuce, tomatoes, and cucumbers. There are many salads with a much wider array of ingredients. Do you remember when you first saw a salad with strawberries on it? It was like a meal and dessert all in one. It seemed to break all the rules of salad. Internships are much like salads. Long gone are the days where interns are merely getting coffee, picking up dry cleaning, and washing the car. Today, with the help a bit from the Federal

Government, internships are usually more substantive. You may still be asked to run and pick up the lunch order for the office, but it should be rare. A common rule I share with my students is up to 20% of your internship tasks may be unrelated to the specific career you are interning for. Yes, you may be copying and answering phones, but this should only happen about 20% or less of the time. Let's put that in perspective. If your internship requires 120 hours of work in the placement, this means that up to about 24 hours may be stapling, copying, filing, answering the phone, and, yes, getting coffee.

TOOLS FOR EXCEEDING IN YOUR INTERNSHIP

Here is a list of resources to watch and read. Each reinforces the topics presented in the chapter.

Taniya Arora (2020): "Business Etiquette"

This article provides a description of business etiquette. Learn what is expected of you as an intern and employee.

WATCH AT https://scicomm.in/business/business-etiquette/

Toggl (n.d.): "21 Business Etiquette Rules You Should Never Break"

This is a great article with additional information on business etiquette, including some rules to follow.

WATCH AT https://toggl.com/track/business-etiquette-rules/

(continued ...)

Indeed (2021): "Guide to Business Attire (With Examples)"

Have an interview? Not sure what to wear? This article discusses the basics of business dress.

WATCH AT https://www.indeed.com/career-advice/starting-new-job/guide-to-business-attire

Indeed (2021): "10 Ways to Get the Most From Your Internship"

This article from Indeed discusses how to gain the most from your internship experience.

WATCH AT https://www.indeed.com/career-advice/starting-new-job/how-to-get-the-most-from-your-internship

CREDIT

IMG 10.1: Copyright © 2012 Depositphotos/michaeljung.

CHAPTER 11

Let's Get Real
What to Expect Upon Graduation

Life after college is what you are working toward. As you work toward your dream job it is easy to lose sight of what life will be like after college. Gone will be the days of classes, filled residence halls, and roommates. Class work will be well over, and the guidance of faculty and staff will be less immediate and visible. As you start your senior year, family and friends will begin to talk about the "real world." Don't think for a minute that you have not been in a real world. You have. Consider college as being just one chapter in the book of your life. Each and every chapter represents real experiences and a real life lived. There are many things to consider and reflect on to be prepared for the transition into the next chapter of your life. This chapter will discuss what to expect upon graduation.

Expectations vs. Reality

When you're dreaming of your future career, what do you see? Probably that dream job and the big paycheck that goes along with it, right? The sad reality of life after college is that your dream job is still probably a few career moves (and salary brackets) away from where you start right after you earn your degree. This may also be true for internships in some cases. You often hear about your classmates landing dream internships. Having these expectations of what your career will look like right out of college is probably what got you through undergraduate studies, but it's hard to be faced with the reality not quite matching up. It's never too late to start thinking about how to get into that first job and to make those connections and those decisions that will set you up for success once you're ready to graduate. Don't let anyone tell you it's too early to prepare, even if it's your first year! Be sure you are meeting with people in your desired industry and having candid conversations about what to expect as a newbie entering the field. Use the following guide to connect with industry professionals.

EXERCISE 11.1
The Connected Professional Project

The purpose of this activity is to connect you with a professional in your desired career field or related field. Being connected with a seasoned professional who has walked the journey on which you are embarking is a valuable opportunity. The structure of this activity is designed to help you make the most of the opportunity.

This experience is a guided experience. Activities and milestones are created to prompt engaging conversations with your connected professional. You may decide to complete it in a single semester or over years.

- Initiate contact with your connected professional; send an introductory email.
- At conclusion of your meeting, discuss and plan for the second Zoom meeting. Send a "thank you" email within 12 hours of completing the meeting.
- At the conclusion of the second meeting, discuss and plan for the third Zoom meeting. Send a "thank you" email within 12 hours of completing the meeting.
- During the third meeting, ask for a referral of another professional who would be willing to meet with you via Zoom. Send a "thank you" email within 12 hours of completing the meeting.
- Repeat this process to effectively grow your professional network. Follow up with previous connections as appropriate. Be sure to manage your relationships.

Conversation Themes for Connected Professional Conversations

Zoom Meeting 1: The Great Narrative
The focus of this meeting will be to learn the journey your connected professional took as they developed their career. You want to learn about their path, using the following questions and discussion prompts:

1. Discuss the college they attended, the degrees they received, their major and minor, clubs they were involved in, sports they played, and so on.
2. What, if any, internships did the professional do while in college?
3. What would they have done differently in college, and why?
4. Who was their favorite faculty, and why?
5. What assignment do they most remember, and why?

(continued ...)

Zoom Meeting 2: Coaching for Skills

The focus of this meeting will be asking for specific information about necessary skills, tools, and competencies for your success in the launching your career. Use the following questions and discussion prompts during your meeting:

1. Share your resumes (traditional and infographic).
2. Ask your connected professional what skills, tools, and competencies are missing on your resume. Discuss why those are important. What role do they play in helping you be successful in your career journey?
3. Discuss different ways the connected professional can suggest for gaining the skills, tools, and competencies.
4. Ask questions regarding how the professional uses specific skills and tools.
5. Practice talking about your skills, tools, and competencies. Ask for feedback.

Zoom Meeting 3: Sage Advice

The focus of this meeting will be learning about the trends of the industry. This conversation is future focused; use the following questions and discussion prompts during your meeting:

1. What trends do they see in the industry, position, company, and so on?
2. Ask for specific resources you could watch or read to learn more about these trends.
3. Other than networking, like you are doing now, what experiences do they recommend, such as shadowing or mentoring? Is there an opportunity for this experience to grows into formal, professional mentoring.
4. Discuss ways you should be networking in the industry.
5. Ask them to share their professional network. Get a referral for another professional who would be willing to speak with you.

Conversation Ideas for Referred Professional Conversation

You will only have one Zoom conversation with the second professional. You will want to take pieces from the outline of themes we've discussed and use them to create a cohesive and engaging conversation. Consider asking the referred professional to recommend another professional to speak with. Keep the networking alive and working.

In the following space describe who or what type of professional you would like to connect with. Also, make some notes on how you may connect with the desired professional. Think about how you could use LinkedIn, conferences, networking events, family, friends, and faculty:

(continued ...)

Target Professional:	Ideas for Connecting:
Target Professional:	**Ideas for Connecting:**
Target Professional:	**Ideas for Connecting:**
Target Professional:	**Ideas for Connecting:**

One of the best things you can do to help manage your expectations versus the reality of your intended industry is to know before you graduate what your earned experience will get you paid. Know what jobs you're qualified for, and do the research to understand the salary range for that level and type of position in the industry. Knowing that you're being paid a fair wage will help take the edge off that disappointment that you're not making six figures right away. If you know that the job will help you advance in your career, then you can also think of it as being one step closer to getting that six-figure salary. And if all else fails, remember that some money is better than no money, if it's a fair wage. Every person has to start someplace. Keep your expectations regarding pay within reason. Do research on the salaries for your state and city.

iMG 11.1

When you're looking for jobs, it's also important to remember that your student loans will come due a lot faster than you think. The grace period (typically 6 months), if you have one, will go by quickly. Keep in mind that you will have that bill to think about as well. While being worried about finances shouldn't be your only deciding factor in what job you take, it's something to remember when you're considering turning down a perfectly good offer because you think someone will pay you more money if you keep looking just a little longer. If you're being offered a wage that will ensure you can pay back your student loans, go for it. There's nothing wrong with keeping your options open, while working a decent job for the paycheck. Keep in mind, although it is not common for communication jobs, some employers will offer student loan repayment assistance or a sign-on bonus. Don't be shy to explore options with the hiring agent.

The gig economy used to be most associated with musicians who accept gigs to play music. Now, it has a broader meaning and refers to freelancing. Freelance work is a great bonus revenue stream, but until you are very established it is not very reliable or consistent. Don't count on freelance money to pay your bills—any of them. There are slow seasons in freelancing when you won't make as much money, if any. Make sure your day job can pay all your bills and necessities, and use that freelance money for discretionary expenses or extra payments on student loans. Freelance work can be a source of portfolio pieces. Start looking at opportunities in your senior year. You might be surprised how many people are looking for project-based hires for speech writing, slide deck design, graphic design, and so on. These projects would be great additions to any student's resume. It would be a bit unexpected but would demonstrate initiative, which most employers seek in new employees. These are all things that probably never even made it into your set of expectations, but they're certainly going to have a big impact on your post-graduation reality.

So how do you deal with the disappointment of not making $60 thousand a year and living on your own right out of college like you dreamt? The first thing to do is acknowledge that you are disappointed. It's okay to be sad that you've worked so hard to chase a dream that's just not reality yet. Just don't dwell on it. Instead, arm yourself with knowledge like the industry data from the first paragraph. This knowledge will give you hope that you will get to live your dream, just in a few years and a few job changes from now. The third thing to do after you've acknowledged your disappointment and done your research is shift your focus from the dream to the reality. Make the choice to love what you're doing now, and rest in the fact that you're doing well for yourself. Make the best of your reality, and you'll feel a lot less down about what you were expecting your life to be like right out of college.

It is helpful to use a budget worksheet during college, especially your senior year, so you have a clear picture of your finances and cost of living expenses. By doing this you are armed with a realistic idea of what base salary you need to live.

SPOTLIGHT ON COMMUNICATION
Constructivism

The theory of constructivism has roots in several other fields including psychology, education, and biology. Swiss philosopher Jean Piaget coined the term "constructivism" (Plus, 2016). This is a theory that focuses on our ability to differentiate the way others make sense of things and to create person-centered messages. Piaget argued that we produce knowledge and create meaning based upon our experiences. Accommodation and assimilation are two components in the process of creating new knowledge. We use assimilation when we incorporate new experiences into the existing or old experiences. As we assimilate, we develop new perspectives. This can have an impactful result on changing our opinions and perceptions or reevaluating misunderstandings. Accommodation takes place when we reframe our experiences into an existing cognitive framework. Each of us sees the world in a certain way. When we experience something that does not align with what we thought, accommodation and reframing occurs.

With the knowledge of constructivism, you can reflect on the connected professional exercise you completed. The process of talking with established professionals in the career or industry you are interested in provides information that will require you to either assimilate or accommodate. Often, I hear students describe their intended careers as contradictory to the reality of those careers. For example, a student might be attracted to public relations because they enjoy talking to others and dislike writing. In reality, public relations is a writing-intensive field. Make use of the opportunities available during your college years to construct helpful, new meanings and perspectives on your intended career and how to be successful in it.

EXERCISE 11.1
Budget Worksheet Activity

In the following budget worksheet, include all expenses, including those other people, like parents, currently pay on your behalf. For example, while in college your parents may agree to pay your car payment. Include your car payment amount in the fixed expenses section, but also include the amount as income from your parent. It would be helpful to remove any external help that will disappear once graduated and settled. Also, note that the cost of tuition and fees are not included in the budget because you will have graduated. If you are doing this while still in college, feel free to add it.

(continued ...)

Income	Daily	Monthly	Semesterly	Yearly
From Jobs After Taxes				
From Parents/Family				
From Financial Aid				
Misc. Income				
Other				
Total Income:				

Fixed Expenses	Daily	Monthly	Semesterly	Yearly
Rent/Housing				
Food/Meal Plan				
Car Payment				
Car Insurance and Registration				
Cell Phone				
Loan/Credit Cards				
Utilities				
Other				
Total Fixed Expenses:				

Flexible Expenses	Daily	Monthly	Semesterly	Yearly
Internet				
Cable/Streaming Services				
Clothes				
Eating Out				
Transportation/Gas				
Entertainment				
Other				
Total Fixed Expenses:				

Savings	Daily	Monthly	Semesterly	Yearly
Long-Term Goals				
Buying a House				
Buying a New Car				
Investing				
Other				
Total Long-Term Savings:				

(continued ...)

	Short-Term Goals			
Vacation				
New Electronics/Phone				
Other				
Totaled Short Term Savings:				

I've placed a lot of emphasis on researching and knowing your industry-standard salary, so you can manage your expectations. There's another benefit to doing that kind of research: knowing the job market. One of the best things you can do is to research what the pay range is in your industry and find where you fall on that spectrum before you apply for positions. Know what you are worth. With that also comes knowing what the market is like in your area and what qualifications you need to fit into that market. Do this research by a specific city or area, rather than by country, for the most accurate results. Each city has its own demand and supply of employees, and the pay scale may look a little different as well. National averages are great for getting a broad idea of what to expect, but nothing will give you a better idea than looking at 10 job listings for a city and finding the average salaries of those jobs.

When you're looking at the job market, you'll probably see many contract or freelance work available. Especially in communications and journalism, there's becoming a lot of emphasis on the gig economy and contract work. The reason for that shift isn't really discussed much. Having contractors or freelancers is less expensive for employers because they don't have to pay for benefits. It's bad for you, though, because you need those benefits. There are also some tax implications you'll want to watch out for. There's nothing wrong with taking that kind of job as long as you're fully aware of the fine print.

All that being said, freelancing within your industry could be a great opportunity to get started in your dream career. It's one more way to make connections and bring in a little extra money on the side. Just make sure it's in addition to your day job. It's certainly not uncommon in the communications industry to meet people who have found their next job through freelance work and have, in the meantime, made thousands from freelance contracts. Know your skills, and flex your degree to get a little extra cash and experience. Remember it can all go on your resume and be added to your portfolio!

The freelance industry provides you the opportunity to make your own opportunities, especially in communications-related fields; the options are endless! If you find yourself looking for a job in something that doesn't exist yet, make it yourself. The business environment is ever-changing, and staying ahead of the trends is likely to be rewarding. There's nothing that says you have to wait for an existing job that's exactly what you're looking for to come around. Remember the roles of social influencer or social media writer did not exist when your parents were your age. It's easier than ever to create your own business and even easier to market yourself. There are so many tools, many free, on the internet. Plus, before graduating look into the resources your campus offers for new start-ups. Most communities have resources for new start-ups and small businesses. Many of these services are free or at a low cost. For example, if you are interested in starting your own business look for an incubator in your community. Small business incubators offer shared office space for new entrepreneurs. They will offer sessions on key topics you will need to know, like how to market your new business.

Even if you are not to the point in your college career that you're looking for jobs, creating your own opportunities will help you develop more than just hard skills for your resume. You will also build perseverance, interpersonal communication skills, confidence in talking with clients and customers, and so much more (Indeed Editorial Team, 2021). The benefits of creating your own opportunities don't stop there. By creating your own opportunities, you are showing faculty and prospective employers you are not afraid to take risks, you know how the industry works, and you are thinking outside the box. You will also have a great way to showcase your talents. If you have a web presence for whatever opportunity you create, link to it in your resume and social media to gain traction and make sure hiring managers and recruiters see it.

Job Hunting

Job hunting is going to be a full-time job for a little while as you're preparing to graduate and move into your field. From doing your job market research to attending interviews, it all takes a lot more time than you think it does. It's time you're not making money, so it's best to plan ahead and get a jump start on the process while you're still in school. To help your search while you're still in college, develop post-internship strategies to secure a job after graduation:

- As for references! Ask anyone you worked with who will speak well of you. Do it before you start applying for jobs, so they're not blindsided, and keep in touch with them after you leave the internship.

- Update your resume once you start a new job.
- Build and maintain a LinkedIn page now that you have some professional.
- Continue to maintain your portfolio! Update it with any clips you're authorized to use from your internship or at least a short description of what you did there. Update your portfolio often, even when you're not looking for jobs.

Another thing you can do while you're in college is develop and hone your people skills. Make meaningful connections with your professors, your peers, and upper classmen. You never know who you could help down the road. Professors and upperclassmen are great resources for finding a job out of college. Professors you're close with may also have contacts to help you find a job or internship. You should also attend networking events hosted by your college and talk to people there, instead of just floating around the room. These are called networking events for a reason! There many recruiters and hiring managers there who are looking for young talent. If you want to go the extra mile, get contact cards made (or make them yourself if you have the skills) to hand out at events, and keep a few in your wallet. Don't be shy about handing these out! They're just like business cards—just for you as a person. Make sure to list your degree path on the card, so whoever you gave it to remembers why they have it.

During your job search, you may be contacted by recruiters. Always reply to them. They will help you with this new full-time job that is looking for paying jobs. It's their job to find talent and place it with the right company. They always seem to reach out when you're least expecting it, which is why it's so important to keep your resume and portfolio up to date, so you can forward them to recruiters when asked. These recruiters tend to reach out when they have a job in mind that you'd be qualified for, and they may or may not be right in their assessment that you're qualified for it. It all depends on how much they know about your field. Nevertheless, maintain a good relationship with them during and after the recruiting process, even if the job does work out. Either way, if they know they're welcome to keep sending you jobs to look at, they'll be a great connection to have. Always remember to thank them for thinking of you and taking the time to reach out to you, and follow up with them after you interview for the job to let them know how it goes. Treat them like a hiring manager at a company, and you'll get pretty far with them. They have a lot of say in how you're presented to the company, as they're the ones pitching you to the real hiring manager.

The world of recruiters can be a little daunting, and it's important not to rely on them for everything, but if you're aware they're a tool in your arsenal, you can cover more ground in your industry a lot faster. If you're really struggling to find positions on your own, reach out to a recruiting company, and ask to be put on their list to be contacted if a certain type of job is available. There's nothing wrong with a little extra help.

The last thing to keep in mind as you're preparing to apply for jobs is that your last month of college will be stressful and may not leave you much time to apply for jobs or attend interviews. So start the search before finals set in, and just be prepared to tell an employer you won't be able to start until after you graduate. They will likely be expecting this and won't mind. Having your dream job lined up and then getting a terrible grade on a final isn't quite the grand entrance you're looking for into your industry. Remember to manage your time well and that applying for jobs is a full-time job, but so are finals.

Keeping Your Head Up

Looking for a job and balancing the loss of what you expected life after graduation to be is hard. It is natural to feel defeated and disillusioned. The transition from college student to working professional is daunting for most students. Remember you are not doing this alone. You have a team of university faculty and staff as well as family and friends, who are all available to assist you in this transition. Change is hard. Change can stir many different emotions. So how do you stay motivated?

One of the best things you can do is to have a plan, and do the next right thing. If you have a clear path forward and stay on it, you will feel much better. Find the little victories on that path, and celebrate those wins to help keep yourself motivated. A little dreaming also doesn't hurt if you are using it to inspire yourself. Research some of the top professionals in the industry and use their career to be inspirational to you. Their success can help you determine short- and long-term goals. Keep in mind your ultimate end goal to motivate yourself to stay on track and keep doing the next right thing. Recognize that very few people are overnight successes. It is unrealistic to put that pressure on yourself. As a young toddler you learned how to walk. You struggled to get up—to stay upright for long. People surrounded you, encouraging you. Even though you fell many times over, no one was discouraging. You were not hard on yourself. Instead, you kept working at it, until you learned how to walk independently. This process of learning something new and working at it until you are successful should be the model you use when launching into your career. Keep this scene playing on repeat in your mind.

If you are feeling defeated because no one is inviting you for interviews, just remember that wallowing won't help as much as another round of job applications. Of course, you may also be feeling a little defeated because you are burning out on completing job applications. Try giving yourself a carrot to finish your daily job-search tasks, hangout with friends, have a special dinner, or take a long nap. Be mindful to take care of yourself as you search for a job. You can also try changing up your environment while you are completing job applications. Just like studying, this really does help give you a fresh burst of energy.

Lastly, when you do not end up getting that job that you interviewed for, change your perspective. Even if you do not get that job, every interview and job application serves as practice for the next one. The same goes for writing cover letters and doing career research. Even if you are starting to feel like it is futile, just remember that practice makes progress, and you learn something from every experience, even if it does not turn out the way you had hoped. This is also a great time to revisit your college campus in person or virtually and connect with faculty and career services. Ask key people to review what you have been doing and offer suggestions for improvements. Keep in mind you did not learn how to walk without help. Why should launching your career be any different? There are no prizes for struggling and not asking for help. It is worth reflecting throughout your job search and asking yourself if you are making it harder that it should be. Reach out and use the services and resources available on your campus and in your community.

When the search has been dragging on for a while, it is easy to give up a little and stop working as hard. Remember that you are in this for the long haul, and you have already dedicated so much time and money to be where you are today. Give yourself a little pep talk or break from the job search as a pick-me-up, but then get back to it. It is not easy, but when you are starting to give up a little bit is when you really need to remind yourself to be relentless in your search for the next right move.

From the first day of your first year of college until you retire, your career should be driven by "relentless intentionality" (Ellison, 2011). Relentless intentionality may sound a little intense, but that is the point. This book is guiding you through the process of being relentlessly intentional about making the most of your degree. Be intentional about the organizations you join, the connections you make, and the courses you take in college. Be relentless in your pursuit of opportunity, new skills, new ideas, and the next right employment opportunity. It all sounds like a lot, but as soon as you change your mindset to being relentlessly intentional as a default, the way you live your life and interact with the world will change. Being relentlessly intentional is a mindset you should carry with you even beyond college and that first job search. Employers will reward your perseverance and drive.

It is important to keep a balance in your life, even when job hunting. Maintain balance between your job search and schoolwork, planning and executing, and work and life. We all hear about work–life balance and how so many professionals are starting to value that more than other benefits provided by their employers. There is something to be learned from that when you are in college. In college, professors do not really teach you about work–life balance, and it's easy to get stuck in the rut of working all the time on school and career-related projects. You are going to have a much harder time keeping your head up for the long haul if you are burnt out and do not have a good balance between working on finding a job and actually living your life. Your life now is never just a transitional moment to get to something better. It has its own benefits and experiences that are valuable, and you should strive to maintain balance. It's also great practice for when you're working a full-time job. Then you will really need a good balance, or you will burn out quickly.

On the topic of balance, it is important to have hobbies that you do not monetize or use to help grow your career. Do not try to turn yourself into a machine because you think it will help you get a better job. It is not worth anything if you are miserable. Make sure you have hobbies that you enjoy, and spend time with friends and family. The little things are important, too (Indeed Editorial Team, 2021). Hobbies give you a way to broaden your horizons and take a break from the, as the internet says, grind of the job search. Carry these hobbies with you into your professional life as something to look forward to on the weekends, as well.

In interview prep, a lot of people will coach you that you will be asked about your hobbies outside of work. This may or may not still be true. It should be because it shows that the employer values having a well-rounded employee. You should have hobbies independent of your career choices just for the health and emotional benefits of a well-rounded life, but it helps to have a response prepared for when you are asked in an interview or even by faculty and other people within your industry about what you like to do outside of the profession. Make sure you have a few hobbies you are passionate about and would be happy to talk about for a few seconds with someone, such as reading, hiking, swimming, or working on cars. Hobbies can be something fun that will help interviewers remember you.

Go Forth and Conquer

You processed a lot of information throughout this book. No doubt, you have received even more advice from faculty, career counselors, and members of the industry. You do not have to follow every bit of advice everyone gives you. In fact, you should not follow advice blindly. Take all the advice you have been given, turn it over, and use it to make a plan and give yourself some direction (MIT Career Advising & Professional Development, n.d.) and activities. Use this book as a tool to work out your career plan throughout your college career and after graduation. Everyone has a path, and this is the time in your life to build yours.

TOOLS FOR POST-GRADUATION EXPECTATIONS

Explore online resources for connecting with a professional, like MeetUp, EventBrite, or national or international networking groups. Following are some examples to get you started.

- **MeetUp:** www.meetup.com
- **EventBrite:** www.eventbrite.com
- **LinkedIn:** www.linkedin.com/feed
- **Quora:** www.quora.com
- **Viadeo:** viadeo.journaldunet.com
- **XING (Germany, Austria, and Switzerland):** www.xing.com/en

There are several websites for exploring freelance work. Some of the most popular sites include the following:

- **Fiverr:** www.fiverr.com
- **UpWork:** www.upwork.com/about/
- **Toptal:** www.toptal.com/

CREDIT

IMG 11.1: Copyright © 2016 Depositphotos/alphaspirit.

GLOSSARY

abstract conceptualization: The abstract conceptualization of the assignment is when you form ideas and theories about the completed or ongoing assignment.

aggressive culture: Aggressive organizational cultures thrive on a spirit of competitiveness and outperforming others.

artifacts: Artifacts are objects or messages that reflect elements of an organization. These may be verbal or nonverbal.

artistic: From John Holland's RIASEC theory, artistic refers to people who are creative and innovative. Common personality traits shared by artistic people include being imaginative, disorderly, idealistic, emotional, and sometimes impractical.

assumptions: Assumptions are part of an organizational culture and refers to the deepest level representing beliefs about reality.

boundaries: The system theory of organizations refer to boundaries to define membership in a system.

bridge questions: Questions that are similar to connecting questions, except the information is being connected to something outside the classroom.

broad values: Often called personal values, these values usually transfer across specific contexts.

business strategy: Business strategy refers to the basic understanding of business processes.

cognitive script: Our brains process information and store it in cognitive files. These files allow us to access information when we need it. A script is a stored memory of how we communicated or performed a previous task. The more often you complete the task the more solid the script becomes and is used repeatedly.

communication collateral: Any message you create to enhance the brand of a company or person—also referred to as marketing collateral. There are many different pieces of collateral. Some examples include social media posts and videos, email, newsletters, presentations, magazines, and white papers.

competitive advantage: Skills, attributes, and experiences that distinguish you from your competitors, such as other applicants, students, and employees.

comprehension questions: A question that seeks further explanation to help you understand the material. This is the most common type of questions students ask in class. When you are seeking clarity about something, you ask for more information.

concrete experience: Experiential learning activities that provide tangible experience represented by demonstrable skills.

connecting questions: A question that helps you link the information with something you previously learned or to another class.

conscious incompetence: Conscious incompetence is making mistakes repeatedly and being aware that you are making the mistakes.

conventional: From John Holland's RIASEC theory conventional career people are known as "organizers."

core values: Principles that guide a person's behavior and their relationship with the world around them. This principle is considered fundamental to what the person sees as being important.

detail-oriented culture: Detail-oriented organizational cultures are characterized as having a competitive advantage over other organizational cultures because of their attention to precision and details.

disciplined people: Author Jim Collins's term that refers to who's "on the bus," or in an organization. Having the right people on the bus and in the right seats is vital to success. In this book you are encouraged to consider the bus as your major and intended career.

enterprising: From John Holland's RIASEC theory, enterprising people are known as "persuaders."

equifinality: Equifinality is part of the system theory or organizations and refers to the different ways of getting to the same result.

experiential learning: A type of learning that involves concrete experience, reflective observation, abstract conceptualization, and active experimentation.

extrinsic values: Tangible rewards you receive from your career. The most common example of an extrinsic reward you receive from work is money or pay.

feedback: Feedback is part of the communication process. It requires communicators to provide verbal or nonverbal response to another's message.

general education: A common core of courses required by universities to earn a bachelor's degree. Usually the general education core consists of core subjects like English; history; science; mathematics; health/fitness; and religion, culture, and a foreign language.

Hierarchy: From the organizational systems theory, hierarchy refers to the layers each system has, which suggests systems are complex.

ideal self: The image of what you wish you were like is your ideal self.

innovative culture: Innovative cultures are characterized by being flexible, adaptable, and experimenting.

interests: The things you have a desire to learn more about or spend more time doing.

intrinsic values: What motivates you internally to do what you do, such as work. When applying core values to your future career, intrinsic values motivate you do the work you do.

investigative: From John Holland's RIASEC theory, investigative people are thinkers. They like to observe, learn, analyze, evaluate, and problem-solve.

knowledge economy: An economy relies on the quantity, quality, and accessibility of information available.

learning objectives: Statements about what a person will learn or wants to learn.

lifestyle values: How you want to live. These values determine your lifestyle.

mentoring: A professional relationship in which one person has more experience and coaches the other person to gain a competitive advantage in the field or job market.

mission statement: A brief statement that describes why an organization exists, its purpose, and its overall goal. It is not uncommon for individual majors, clubs, and even special events in colleges to have a mission statement.

occupational outlook handbook: A publication of the U.S Department of Labor's Bureau of Labor Statistics that is a collection of information about different occupations. The descriptions of the occupations include the nature of work, working conditions, training and education, earnings, and job outlook.

organizational culture: Shared assumptions, values, and beliefs of employees.

organizational systems theory: Systems theory is an approach to studying organization as a set of interdependent parts, each with its own specific function and interrelated responsibilities.

outcome-oriented culture: Outcome-oriented cultures place priority on results and achievements. This type of organization is often very dynamic and may have high a turnover of employees.

people-oriented culture: People-oriented organizational cultures ascribe to a human relations model of management, which places value on fairness, supportiveness, and respecting individual rights as priorities.

personal brand: An intentional effort to mold the perception of others, specifically prospective employers and colleagues, by showcasing skills and expertise that differentiates you from others (competitors). The goal of a personal brand is to raise your potential impact within your desired career industry.

portfolio: A collection of work that serves as evidence of skills and expertise. A portfolio might be a hard copy or electronic.

power skills: General skills, such as problem-solving, effective communication, analyzing information and thinking independently, that are basic skills necessary for job success. Power skills are not discipline-specific skills.

realistic: From John Holland's RIASEC theory, realistic people are doers. Realistic people are likely prefer physical activities requiring skills, strength, and often coordination.

reflective observation: Reflective observation is processes information about an experience.

relational network mapping: A record of people you have worked with and experiences, milestones, turning points, and so on worth remembering.

RIASEC theory: John Holland, a psychologist, developed a theory that suggests people can be described as having six personality types. The personality types include realistic, investigative, artistic, social, enterprising, and conventional.

self: The self is the way in which you view yourself that is co-constructed with and through our social enviornoment.

self-esteem or self-worth: Self-esteem or self-worth is the value you place on yourself. This is one of three parts that make up your self-concept.

self-image: Self-image is your view of oneself and is one of three parts that make up your self-concept.

skills: The things you are able to do well. Having skill at something usually means you have some level of expertise.

skills gap: The missing skills required by a certain job or industry. To determine your skills gap compare the list of skills on your resume with the "must have" skills listed in advertised open positions for a job. If the job is asking for something you do not have on your resume, there is a gap.

small group development: Most commonly refers to the five stages a group goes through as the people work together. The five stages are known as forming, storming, norming, performing, and adjourning.

SMART goals: Goals that are specific, measurable, attainable, relevant, and time based.

SMARTE goals: An extension of SMART goals. The most effective goals should be elevating. The goals you set and achieve should elevate you to a new place in your career (and life).

social: From John Holland's RIASEC theory, social people are helpers. Social people like to work with people and even may have an interest in healing or developing others.

stable culture: Stable organizational cultures are characterized by being predictable and rule-governed. There tends to be several layers in the hierarchy. Organizations take comfort in stability and find that this brings more consistent results.

SWOT analysis: A business tool that helps analyze a specific idea, organization, situation, and so on. SWOT stands for examining four components of a specific idea: strengths, weaknesses, opportunities, and threats.

team-oriented culture: Team-oriented organizational cultures are characterized as placing an emphasis on employee collaboration and cooperation. Employees often play a role in evaluating colleagues. There is a sense among employees across all levels of the hierarchy that a positive relationship with each other is vital for a successful workplace.

think tank: A body of experts who provide research, advice and recommendations on specific social issues, political problems, and economic problems. The most influential think tanks in the USA include the Belfer Center for Science and International Affairs, the Earth Institute, the Heritage Foundation, the Human Rights Watch, the Kaiser Family Foundation, the Council on Foreign Relations, the American Enterprise Institute, the RAND Corporation, and the Center for Strategic and International Studies.

unconscious incompetence: When you unknowingly making small mistakes.

Values: A set of principles or standards that guides a person's behaviors. Values are judgments of what is important to a person, and they influence how one lives and works.

values: A general term referring to a person's belief of how one should behave. It also reflects what the person views as being important in life or work.

video cover letter: A brief, no longer than 2-minute video that allows you address prospective employers, introducing them to your work experience and overall fit with the prospective job.

REFERENCES

7 Industry Experts Give Their Top Tips for Public Relations Graduates. (2017, March 16). Harrington Communications & Content. http://katieharrington.ie/312-2/

2018 Strada-Gallup Alumni Survey. (2018). Gallup. https://news.gallup.com/reports/244058/2018-strada-gallup-alumni-survey.aspx

Appleby, D. (2017). *The soft skills students need to succeed now and in the future.* American Psychological Association. https://www.apa.org/ed/precollege/psn/2017/09/soft-skills.

Arruda, W. (2016). *The most damaging myth about branding.* Forbes. https://www.forbes.com/sites/williamarruda/2016/09/06/the-most-damaging-myth-about-branding/?sh=2c7ec62e5c4f

Bradford, L. (2018). *Why all employees need data skills in 2019 (and beyond).* Forbes. https://www.forbes.com/sites/laurencebradford/2018/10/11/why-all-employees-need-data-skills-in-2019-and-beyond/?sh=1e94453510f6

Brooks, R. (2018). Workplace Spotlight: What Google Gets Right about Company Culture, *Peakon.* https://web.archive.org/web/20200925145237/https://peakon.com/us/blog/workplace-culture/google-company-culture/

Burch, J. (2021). *Three out of four firing managers look up your social media profiles: Are you ready?* Pro Resume Center, LLC. https://www.proresumecenter.com/three-out-of-four-hiring-managers-look-up-your-social-media-profiles-are-you-ready/

Bureau of Labor Statistics. (2022). Field of degree: Communications. https://www.bls.gov/ooh/field-of-degree/communications/communications-field-of-degree.htm

Carroll, L. (2018). *Alice in Wonderland.* Wordsworth Editions.

Cengage Group. (2021). *New Cengage report finds recent college graduates feel underqualified to enter the workforce.* https://www.cengagegroup.com/news/press-releases/2021/new-cengage-report-finds-recent-college-graduates-feel-underqualified-to-enter-the-workforce/

Center for First Generation Student Sucess(n.d.) *Center for first generation Student Success.* https://firstgen.naspa.org/about-the-center

Coca-Cola (n.d.) *Brands.* https://www.coca-colacompany.com/brands

Cole, N. (2019). *How sociologists define human agency.* ThoughtCo. https://www.thoughtco.com/agency-definition-3026036

Collins, J. (2001, October). *Good to Great.* Jim Collins. https://www.jimcollins.com/article_topics/articles/good-to-great.html#articletop

Curtiss, P. R., & Warren, P. W. (1973). *The dynamics of life skills coaching. Life skills series.* Prince.

Disney (n.d.) About. https://thewaltdisneycompany.com/about/#:~:text=Our%20Mission,the%20world's%20premier%20entertainment%20company.

Dudovskiy, J. (2021). *Apple SWOT analysis.* Business Research Methodology. https://research-methodology.net/apple-swot-analysis/

Dwyer, M. & Peters, C. (2021). *The benefits of study abroad.* IES Abroad. https://www.iesabroad.org/news/benefits-study-abroad#sthash.HlOwxWjn.dpbs

Ellison, J. (2011, May 24). *The secret to job search success: Persistence, patience and positivity.* Exhibit City News. https://exhibitcitynews.com/the-secret-to-job-search-success-persistence-patience-and-positivity-2206/

Esposito, E. (2015). The essential guide to writing S.M.A.R.T. goals. *Smartsheet.* https://www.smartsheet.com/blog/essential-guide-writing-smart-goals

Eswara, P. (2019). *Developing your teamwork skills.* Insider Higher Ed. https://www.insidehighered.com/advice/2019/01/28/grad-students-need-improve-their-teamwork-skills-become-more-attractive-employers

Fahad, M. (2016). *Cola wars—Case study.* Medical News Today. https://www.medicalnewstoday.com/articles/310909

Fern, J. (2015). *How to intern: The do's and don'ts of interning* [Video]. YouTube. https://www.youtube.com/watch?v=l78kYyqw_1M

Forbes (2019, December 30). *Council post: 12 top tips for professionals just starting in communications.* https://www.forbes.com/sites/forbescommunicationscouncil/2019/12/30/12-top-tips-for-professionals-just-starting-in-communications/?sh=72286f28300a

Forbes (2019, January 08). *Council post: Considering a communications career? 13 tips for industry newcomers.* https://www.forbes.com/sites/forbescommunicationscouncil/2019/01/07/considering-a-communications-career-13-tips-for-industry-newcomers/?sh=6e794e861731

Forbes Coaches Panel. (2018, October 27). *13 clear signs your job isn't the right fit for you.* Forbes. https://www.forbes.com/sites/forbescoachescouncil/2018/10/26/13-clear-signs-your-job-isnt-the-right-fit-for-you/?sh=29e63bb744a3

Frank, T (2017, May 2). How to build a good relationship with your professor (No. 157) [Audio podcast episode]. In *The College Info Geek Podcast.* College Info Geek. https://collegeinfogeek.com/how-to-build-relationship-with-professor/

Generation Texas (GenTX). (2021). *Events*. http://gentx.org/events/gentxmonth/

Goffman, E. (1959). *The presentation of self in everyday life*. Bantam Doubleday Dell Publishing Group.

Google Students. (2013). *Meet Alyx, a Google sales intern* [Video]. YouTube. https://www.youtube.com/watch?v=cP2fsFpAcig

Grand Canyon University. (2020). *Top 3 advantages to earning a communications degree*. https://www.gcu.edu/blog/language-communication/3-advantages-of-communications-degree

Graybeal, L. (2017). *Management theory of Henry Mintzberg basics*. Business.com. https://www.business.com/articles/management-theory-of-henry-mintzberg-basics/

Hanbury, M. (2018). *Zara is part of the biggest fashion company in the world. Meet the other brands it owns*. Business Insider India. https://www.businessinsider.in/Zara-is-part-of-the-biggest-fashion-company-in-the-world-Meet-the-other-brands-it-owns-/articleshow/66092742.cms

Hansen, P. (2013). *Embrace the shake*. TED. https://www.ted.com/talks/phil_hansen_embrace_the_shake

Hart Research Associates. (2015). *2015 survey report 2 GE trends*. AACU. https://www.aacu.org/sites/default/files/files/LEAP/2015_Survey_Report2_GEtrends.pdf

Hecht, M. L., Warren, J. R., Jung, E., & Krieger, J. L. (2005). A Communication Theory of Identity: Development, Theoretical Perspective, and Future Directions. In W. B. Gudykunst (Ed.), *Theorizing about intercultural communication* (pp. 257–278). Sage Publications Ltd.

Holland, J. (1997). Making vocational choices: A theory of vocational personalities and work environments (3rd ed.). Psychological Assessment Resources.

Indeed Editorial Team. (2021, May 24). *14 career advice tips for college students*. Indeed Career Guide. https://www.indeed.com/career-advice/career-development/career-advice-for-college-students

Indeed. (2020). *Top 11 skills employers look for in candidates*. https://www.indeed.com/career advice/resumes-cover-letters/skills-employers-look-for

Indeed. (2021). *17 traits employers seek in candidates*. https://www.indeed.com/career-advice/finding-a-job/traits-employers-look-for

Indeed. (2021). Transferable skills: Definitions and examples. https://www.indeed.com/careeradvice/resumes-cover-letters/transferable-skills

Jacimovic, D. (2021, March 30). 30 memorable first generation college student statistics. What to Become. https://whattobecome.com/blog/first-generation-college-studentstatistics/

Jacimovic, D. (2021, May 18). 29 astonishing interview statistics. What to Become. https://whattobecome.com/blog/interview-statistics.

Jeffrey, S. (n.d.). *A complete guide to self-actualization: 5 key steps to accelerate growth.* Scott Jeffrey. https://scottjeffrey.com/self-actualization/

Jurevicius, O. (2021). *SWOT analysis of apple (5 key strengths in 2021).* Strategic Management Insight. https://strategicmanagementinsight.com/swot-analyses/apple-swot-analysis/

Katz, D., & Kahn, R. L. (1966). *The social psychology of organizations.* John Wiley and Sons.

Kennelly, S., & Reardon (2018). RIASEC literature from 1953–2016: Bibliographic references to Holland's theory, research, and applications, career developments (technical report no. 58). Florida State University. https://career.fsu.edu/sites/g/files/upcbnu746/files/TR-%2058.pdf

Leary, M. R., & Kowalski, R. M. (1990). Impression management: A literature review and two component model. *Psychological Bulletin, 107,* 34–47.

Make a Career Plan. (n.d.). MIT Career Advising and Professional Development. https://capd.mit.edu/explore-careers/career-first-steps/make-career-plan

Menaker, M. B. (2017, January 11). 10 New Year's resolutions to supercharge your career. The Undercover Recruiter. https://theundercoverrecruiter.com/supercharge-your-career/

Meng, H. (2008). Social script theory and cross-cultural communication. *Intercultural Communication Studies, XVII,* 1.

Miller, C., & Poston, M. (2020). *Exploring communication in the real world.* Pressbooks. https://cod.pressbooks.pub/communication/chapter/13-2-small-group-development/

National Communication Association. (2022). *Why study communication?* National Communication Association. https://www.natcom.org/academic-professional-resources/why-study-communication

NatpeEd. (2008). *Internships & networking* [Video]. YouTube. https://www.youtube.com/watch?v=Lql7lwf7M6A

Nichols, M (Director) (1988). *Working Girl* [Film]. 20th Century Fox.

Nightingale, E. (2020). *41 quests of earl nightingale on success.* The Inspiring Journal. https://www.theinspiringjournal.com/41-earl-nightingale-quotes-on-success/.

Ohio State University. (n.d.). *Major decisions: Facts & figures about students changing majors.* University Explorations. http://exploration.osu.edu/Breaking%20Up%20Is%20Hard%20to%20Do/Changing%20Majors%201.14.pdf

Peart, N. (2019). *Making work less stressful and more engaging for your employees.* Harvard Business Review. https://hbr.org/2019/11/making-work-less-stressful-and-more-engaging-for-your-employees

Plus, O., 2016. *Piaget's theory on constructivism*. Teach-nology. http://www.teach-nology.com/currenttrends/constructivism/piaget/

Principles of management. (2010). University of Minnesota Libraries Publishing. https://open.lib.umn.edu/principlesmanagement/

Princeton Review. (2022). *Top 10 college majors*. https://www.princetonreview.com/collegeadvice/top-ten-college-majors

Trinity University (2021). *Programs & Initiatives*. https://www.trinity.edu/directory/departments-offices/diversity-and-inclusion/programs-initiatives

Purdue University. (2022). *The career closet*. https://www.cco.purdue.edu/Students/WhatWeOffer?tab=CareerCloset

Rogers, C. (1959). A theory of therapy, personality and interpersonal relationships as developed in the client-centered framework. In S. Koch (ed.), *Psychology: A study of a science. Vol. 3: Formulations of the person and the social context*. McGraw Hill.

Saskatchewan, A. (1973). *Training Research and Development Station*. Department of Manpower and Immigration.

Schein, E. H. (1990). Organizational culture. *American Psychologist, 45(2)*, 109–119.

Senge, P., Kleiner, A., Roberts, C., Ross, R., Roth, G., & Smith, B. (1999). *The dance of change: The challenges of sustaining momentum in learning organizations*. Doubleday/Currency.

Shastri, A. (2022). Detailed SWOT analysis of ZARA—World's largest fast fashion brand. IIDE. https://iide.co/case-studies/swot-analysis-of-zara/

Sherman, S. (2021, May 8). *10 leadership strategies to 'crawl, walk, run' your way to success*. Doing CX Right. https://doingcxright.com/2020/09/27/ten-leadership-strategies-to-crawl-walk-run-your-way-to-success/

Society for Human Resource Management. (2013). The cost of poor communication. SHRM. https://www.shrm.org/ResourcesAndTools/hr-topics/behavioral-competencies/communication/Pages/The-Cost-of-Poor-Communications.aspx

Statista. (2019). *Number of higher education institutions in the United States from 1980 to 2017*. Statista. https://www.statista.com/statistics/240833/higher-education-institutions-in-the-us-by-type/

Stoll, J. (2020, May 15). Corporate America's most underrated innovation strategy: 3M's 15% rule. *Wall Street Journal*.

Suzuno, M. (2020, June 19). *5 ways to determine if a company is right for you*. The Muse. https://www.themuse.com/advice/5-fast-ways-to-figure-out-if-a-companys-right-for-you-or-if-you-should-back-away-slowly

Terrell, K. (January 14, 2021). 5 ways the pandemic has changed job hunting. AARP. https://www.aarp.org/work/job-search/info-2021/pandemic-job-hunting-changes.html

The HR Gurus. (2018, July 30). The Indispensable Employee. hrgurus. https://www.hrgurus.com.au/the-indispensable-employee

Tretina, K. (2016). *How to use snapchat in your job search*. WiseBread. https://www.wisebread.com/how-to-use-snapchat-in-your-job-search

Tufts University Career Services. (n.d.). *Interest checklist*. https://cdn.careers.tufts.edu/wpcontent/uploads/sites/100/2020/07/Interests-Checklist.pdf

U.S. Department of Education. (2017). Beginning college students who change their majors within years of enrollment. *Data Point, NCES 2018–434*. https://nces.ed.gov/pubs2018/2018434.pdf

Vora, T. (2010). Great quotes: Be a yardstick of quality. QASPIRE. https://qaspire.com/2010/07/09/great-quotes-be-a-yardstick-of-quality/

INDEX

A
abstract conceptualization, 149, 160, 191
academic advisors, 14
accreditation requirements, 125
adapting to change, 37
Adobe Portfolio, 42
advice, 109, 189–190
   from industry, 135–144
after graduation experiences, 2
agents, 8–9
aggressive culture, 103
Alice in Wonderland (Carroll), 22
Allies First-Generation, 110
Arora, Taniya, 175
artifacts, 102–103
artistic persons
   communication careers, 31
   personality traits, 31
Association for Women in Communications, 25
assumptions, 102
automated scheduling tools, 62
average undergraduate student, 5

B
bachelor's degree, 6, 21, 84, 100
Baden-Powell, Robert, 123
Behance, 41
Bezos, Jeff, 54
boundaries, 132
bridge questions, 12
Britten, Scott, 121–122
budget worksheet activity, 182–184
business strategy, 35
bus metaphor of organizations
   bus driver, 124–127
   choosing right bus, 127–130

C
career choices, 29
   case study, 97–101
career fairs, 112, 139, 152, 155

career goals, 5, 30, 61, 126, 128, 156. *See also* goals of college education
career journey
   bus metaphor, 124–125
   choosing a major, 124–125
   minors and double majors, 127
   resources, 132–133
   shift in destinations, 126
Career Resources for College Students With Disabilities, 49
career success, 22
Cechova, Dominika, 94
chamber of commerce, 148
Chartered Management Institute, 106
Citizen Bank, 17
Clark, Dorie, 68
cognitive script, 10
Cohan, Deborah J., 122
college experiences, 5–6
Collins, Jim, 123–124. *See also* bus metaphor of organizations
   ~Good to Great~, 123–124
communication collateral, 42
communication degree, 5
   advantages of, 102–106
   majors, 11
   resources, 106
competence communicator, 41
competency, 43
competitive advantage of general education, 8–14
comprehension questions, 12
concrete experience, 149
Confucius, 27
Connected Professional Project, 178–180
connecting questions, 12
conscious incompetence, 43
constructive feedback, 136
constructivism, 135–136, 182
conventional people
   careers, 33
   personality traits, 33
core values, 23
   assessment of, 24

Coroflot, 42
COVID-19 pandemic, 37, 77, 93, 143, 152
creative thinking, 47
creators, 31
Crevado, 42
cultures
   aggressive, 103
   detailed-oriented, 103
   innovative, 103
   outcome-oriented, 103
   people-oriented, 103
   stable, 103
   team-oriented, 103
CUNY Internship Programs Intern Handbook, 159
Cutts, Matt, 16

D

data analysis, 42–44
detailed-oriented culture, 103
Digimind, 63
disciplined people, 125
distributive program, 8
doers, 29–30
Dribbble Meetups, 42
Dwyer, Mary, 118

E

edX data analysis and statistics courses, 43
emotional intelligence (EQ), 115
Endresen, Janice, 143
enterprising people, 32
   communication careers, 32
   personality traits, 30
episodic function, 10
equafinality, 131
Eswara, Pallavi, 115
EventBrite, 190
expectations vs reality, 177–178, 180–185
experiential learning, 149–150
Exploring Communication in the Real World, 39
extrinsic values, 24

F

Facebook, 61–63
face-to-face mentors, 15
feedback, 132
Fiverr, 190
Foursquare, 63
Fox, Michelle, 18

freelance work, 181, 184–185
free portfolio services, 42
freshman year, 7

G

gamification, 116
general education
   advantages, 9, 11–12
   as foundation for critical thinking and transferable skills, 7
   classes, 11–12
   competitive advantage in, 8–14
   courses, 6–7
   curriculum, 8, 14
   distributive program, 8
   hybrid model, 8
   influencers, 8–9
   integrative approach, 8
   requirements, 6–8
general education courses, 6
General Electric, 61
Generation Texas (GenTX), 110
getting involved, 121
goals of college education, 7. *See also* SWOT analysis
   resources, 94
   SMARTE goals, 74
   SMART goals, 73–74
Google, 55
Google+, 63
Google Analytics, 42
Griffith, Melanie, 91
grit, 116

H

Hansen, Phil, 26, 48
Heffernan, Margaret, 16
helpers, 31–32
hierarchy, 131
hierarchy of competence model, 43
higher education, 8, 109
Holland Code (RIASEC) Test, 48
Holland, John, 29. *See also* job personality and work environment types
Hootsuite, 62–63
HubSpot Goldman Sachs, 61

I

ideal self, 47
identity, 46–47
IEEE Professional Communication Society, 25

impression management, 166-167
Indeed, 176-177
indivual SWOT analysis, 80-89
innovative culture, 103
interests, 21-22, 26-29
　identifying, 27-28
　influencers shaping, 27
　working with, 33-34
International Association of Business Communicators, 25
international experiences, 118-119
internships, 2, 119
　advantages of, 147-148, 148-149
　applying for, 152-156
　career fairs and, 155
　common questions asked during, 158
　handbooks, 159
　internet sources for, 153-154
　"must dos", 161-175
　nature of, 151-152
　preparing for, 156-158
　resources, 175-176
interpersonal communication, 27, 185
interviews at organization, 104-106
intrinsic values, 23, 26
investigative people, 30-31
　communication careers, 30-31
　personality traits, 30
investing in others, 117-118

J
job applications, 187-188
job hunting/job search, 66, 185-187, 189
job interview preparation and expectations, 119-120
job opening hashtags, 61
job personality and work environment types
　artistic category, 31
　conventional category, 33
　enterprising category, 32
　investigative category, 30-31
　realistic category, 29-30
　social category, 31-32
Jobs, Steve, 60

K
Kinesis, Inc., 133
knowing yourself, 21
"knowledge and application" journal, 11
knowledge economy, 37
Kraft, Dave, 133

L
leadership, 40-41
learning objectives, 149-151
learning organization theory, 110
lifelong career, 21
lifestyle values, 24, 26
Lindstaedt, Bill, 49
LinkedIn, 55, 61-63, 65, 67, 81, 112, 144, 148, 152, 166, 179, 186, 190
Lucier, Kelci Lynn, 106

M
Marian, Peter, 119
mass communication, 27
McCapra, Alastair, 140-141
McKinsey Global Institute, 143
meaningful questions, practice of asking, 13
Medel, Ismael Lopez, 117-118
MeetUp, 190
memory, 116
Menaker, Mandy, 136
mentoring, 15
Miller-Adams, Michelle, 122
mission statement, 58, 124
MITx, 43
Monmouth College's Department of Communication Studies, 67
motivational abilities, 115

N
narrative theory, 158-159
National Association of Crisis Organization Directors, 25
National Career Development Association, 48
National Communication Association, 25
Nation Association of Broadcasters, 25
networking, 154
networking events, 186
Nightingale, Earl, 6

O
occupational outlook handbook, 100-101
oral communication, 41-42
organizational communication, 27
organizational culture, 102-104, 173
　interviews at organization, 104-106
organizational success, 129
organizational systems theory, 131-132
organizers, 33
outcome-oriented culture, 103

P

Pantzalis, Ioannis, 114–116, 119–120
peer mentors, 15
people-oriented culture, 103
personal brand
    attributes with, 59
    creating, 53–60, 115–116
    elaboration likelihood model, 55
    name brand, 54
    significance of, 54
    visual representation, 59
personal SWOT analysis, 89–91
Peters, Courtney K., 118
Peters, Tom, 68
Pi Eta, Lambda, 16–17
Polk State College Internship Handbook, 159
Ponzar, Amanda, 137–138
portfolios, 66–67
    students', 67
power skills, 8
problem-solving skills, 37–39
professional mentors, 15
professional relationship, 56
Public Relations Society of America, 25
public speaking skills training, 32

Q

Quora, 190

R

"rabbit hole" idea, 37
Reade, Colby, 139
realistic individuals, 29–30
    communication careers, 30
    personality traits, 30
reflective observation, 149
relational network mapping, 56–57
relentless intentionality, 188
resources, 67–68, 175–176
    about career, 16–18
    advice from industry, 143–144
    for advice, 122–123
    for connecting with a professional, 190
    for exploring freelance work, 190
    for gaining insight in yourself, 48–49
    for students, 109–111
    internships, 159, 175–176
    SMART Goals, 94
    SWOT analysis, 94
Rhynard, Paul, 142
RIASEC theory, 29
Roberts, Candace A., 119

S

Salazar, Leslie Ramos, 111–113, 120
Schofield, Kerry, 106
30-second elevator pitch plan, 155
Schwabel, Dan, 68
self concept, 46–47
self-confidence, 157
self-discovery, 6, 13, 21
self-esteem, 47
self-image, 47
self-worth, 47
semester or quarter credits, 6
Sherman, Satcy, 138
Shirley, Greg, 17
situational awareness, 40
skills, 21–22, 34–35
    acquisition of, 117
    adaptability, 37
    business strategy, 35
    communication, 41–42
    data analysis, 42–44
    expectations, 121–122
    gap analysis, 44–46
    leadership, 40–41
    problem-solving, 37–39
    teamwork, 39–40
    time management, 35–37
    transferable, 35, 43
small group development, 39
SMARTE goals, 74
SMART goals, 73–74
Snapchat, 61
social media, 60–65
    as stress reliever, 62
    benefits, 61
social people, 31–32
    communication careers, 31–32
    personality traits, 31
social roles, 10
Sprout Social, 63
Squarespace, 41
stable culture, 103
strategic communication, 92
SWOT analysis, 75–93, 126
    Apple, 78–79
    Coca-Cola, 75–76
    of college students, 80–89
    personal, 89–91
    resources, 94
    Zara, 77–78

T

Taco Bell, 61
tactics and best practices for internships, 161–175

adapt to business culture, 173-174
asking of comprehension questions, 170-171
exploring specific industries, 174
finding opportunities to shine, 172-173
first impression, 162-166
learning objectives, 169
make connections, 166
professional approach, 168
requirements of assignments and projects, 170
taking notes, 172
team-oriented culture, 103
teamwork, 39-40
and communication, 113-115
Terenzio, Charlie, 141
thinkers, 30-31
time management skills, 35-37
Toggl, 175
Toptal, 190
transferable skills, 35, 43
TweetDeck, 62
Twitter, 61-63

U
uncertainty, 21-22
unconscious incompetence, 43
Underrepresented Students Program, 110
University of South Florida Internship Handbook, 159
UpWork, 190

V
values, 21-22, 102
  core, 23
  definition, 23
  extrinsic, 24, 26
  in company's mission statement, 58
  influencing career choice, 32-33
  intrinsic, 23, 26
  lifestyle, 24, 26
  noncore, 25
  personal, 25
Viadeo, 190
video cover letter, 65-66

W
Wapnick, Emilie, 17
Wax, Dustin, 122
Weber State University's Department of Communication, 67
Weebly, 41
Whealon, Lisa, 132
Wix, 41
WordPress, 63
work, as socialization agent, 8
Working Girl, 91
working relationship with faculty, 112-113
workplace-ready graduate, 1
Wozniak, Tom, 140
written communication, 41-42

X
XING, 190

Y
Young, Cory, 111, 113

www.ingramcontent.com/pod-product-compliance
Lightning Source LLC
LaVergne TN
LVHW080312260326
834688LV00038B/1072